Gerontology in Theological Education: Local Program Development

Gerontology in Theological Education: Local Program Development

Barbara Payne, PhD
Earl D. C. Brewer, PhD
Editors

The Haworth Press
New York • London

Gerontology in Theological Education: Local Program Development has also been published as *Journal of Religion & Aging*, Volume 6, Numbers 3/4 1989.

The Haworth Press, Inc., 10 Alice Street, Binghamton, NY 13904-1580
EUROSPAN/Haworth, 3 Henrietta Street, London WC2E 8LU England

Library of Congress Cataloging-in-Publication Data

Gerontology in theological education. Local program development / Barbara Payne, Earl D.C. Brewer, guest editors.
    p. cm.
    "'Gerontology in theological education: local program development' has also been published as 'Journal of religion & aging,' volume 6, numbers 3/4, 1989"—T.p. verso.
    Includes bibliographical references.
    ISBN 0-86656-958-8
    1. Church work with the aged—Study and teaching (Graduate)—United States. 2. Gerontology—Study and teaching (Graduate)—United States. 3. Theology—Study and teaching—United States. 4. Aging—Religious aspects—Christianity—Study and teaching (Graduate)—United States. I. Payne, Barbara P. II. Brewer, Earl D. C.
BV4435.G472   1989
261.8'3426'071173—dc20
                                                89-37874
                                                  CIP

Gerontology
in Theological Education:
Local Program Development

CONTENTS

ABOUT THE EDITORS

Barbara Payne, PhD, is Professor of Sociology and Director of the Gerontology Center at Georgia State University in Atlanta. Past President of the Association for Gerontology in Higher Education, Dr. Payne is also the first president and founder of the Southern Gerontological Society. Her publications related to religion and aging include three books: *The Meaning and Measurement of Commitment to the Church, Love in the Later Years*, and *The Protestant Parish*.

Earl D. C. Brewer, PhD, MDiv, is Charles Howard Candler Professor Emeritus of Sociology and Religion, Candler School of Theology, Emory University, Atlanta, Georgia. In the mid-1970s, he was part of the Gerontology in Seminary Training (GIST) project of the National Interfaith Coalition on Aging (NICA). He also serves as an adjunct faculty member of the Gerontology Center at Georgia State University.

Acknowledgements

This project would not have been possible without the colleague-ship and cooperation of many persons. To name a few is to miss many who contributed.

This volume reports on the Atlanta experience in the project. The three seminaries in Atlanta joined in a year-long program of curriculum development and instruction. Special thanks go to the seminary deans: Jim L. Waits of Candler School of Theology, Emory University; Oscar J. Hussel, Columbia Theological Seminary; and David T. Shannon, Interdenominational Theological Center.

A study of library resources was headed by Lynn Thaxton and involved the librarians of the seminaries.

One person from each seminary served the project as a post-doctoral fellow: Drs. Nancy Ammerman, Candler School of Theology, Emory University; Edward Trimmer, Columbia Theological Seminary; and Thomas Pugh, Interdenominational Theological Center.

The fall curriculum was led by Drs. Delmas Allen, Angie Benham, Charles Pyles, and the directors of the project. Other guest faculty included Sheldon Tobin, Editor-in-Chief of *The Gerontologist*; Betsy Styles, Executive Director of the Northside Shepherd's Center; Tom Robb, Director of the Presbyterian Office of Aging; and Joe Whitwell, Director of Psychosocial Services at the Wesley Woods Center.

The spring curriculum involved many faculty persons from the seminaries: Nancy Ammerman, Roberta Bondi, Fred Craddock, James Fowler, Charles Gerkin, Carol Newsom, David Pacini, Theodore Runyon, and Richard Ward from the Candler School of Theology, Emory University; Charles Cousar, Catherine Gonzalez, Wade Huie, Oscar Hussel, Ben Johnson, Jasper Keith, Ben Kline, Lucy Rose, Edward Trimmer, and Christine Wenderoth from the Columbia Theological Seminary; Isaac R. Clark, Melva Costen, Michael Dash, Jacquelyn Grant, Kenneth Henry, Johnathan Jackson, Thomas Pugh, Abraham Smith, and George Thomas from the Interdenominational Theological Center; and Lindsey Pherigo from the St. Paul School of Theology. Major contributions were made by those whose articles appear in this volume.

We are indebted to the entire Georgia State University Gerontology Center staff: to Brooks McLamb for his skilled fiscal management and editing of the publications; to Virginia Erhardt for research assistance and editing; to Barbara Patterson for the long hours and careful attention to the preparation of the three manuscripts; to Najah Head for assistance in the preparation of the manuscripts and supervision of the myriad additional tasks and activities in the center caused by the project; to Adria Alston-Wheeler for her good humored willingness to help each of us with our "project" needs.

Other members of Georgia State University have provided services and support. Special mention should go to Clyde W. Faulkner, Dean of the College of Arts and Sciences; and Mr. Clyde Appling, Director of Grants and Contracts.

Last but not least has been the guidance and support from the Administration on Aging throughout the project. Mrs. Sue Wheaton has been especially helpful.

Barbara Payne, PhD
Earl D. C. Brewer, PhD

Introduction

This is the second in a two-part report on the project on Gerontology in Theological Education (GITE) supported by the Administration on Aging.

The first part provided a national picture of the role of gerontological studies in the curricula of seminaries. It included an introduction to both parts and suggestions and implications for use of the material by seminaries and others interested in religion and aging. There was a report on a national study of seminaries, seven innovative programs in gerontology in theological schools and an annotated bibliography.

This part reports on the experience in Atlanta of the Gerontology Center of Georgia State University working together with the three seminaries to explore options and possibilities for gerontology in theological education. This includes information about the three seminaries and the Gerontology Center, the reports of post-doctoral fellows in gerontology from each seminary, and presentations on aging in various theological disciplines and clergy practices.

Together, these two parts provide a source book for administrators and faculty in theological schools who are concerned about the increasing number of older persons in congregations and communities. There are theoretical, theological and practical materials aimed at providing guidance for those interested in adventuring into aging curricula for the first time or in evaluating and revisioning present commitments.

The summaries have been provided by the Editors.

PART 1: THE ATLANTA EXPERIENCE

The locale of this project was Atlanta. In 1986 the National Meeting of the Association of Gerontology in Higher Education was in Atlanta. Under the leadership of David Oliver of Saint Paul Seminary, there was a preconference session of around 50 persons with concerns for the elderly in theological curriculum. The first presentation was by Jim L. Waits, the Dean of the Candler School of Theology of Emory University. He dealt with the issue of integrating gerontology into seminary curriculum. This is the first article in this section.

The cooperative experiences of the three seminaries and the gerontology center were traced as background to the current project by the codirectors.

This was followed by the reports of the three post-doctoral fellows representing the seminaries.

These three articles provide an introduction to the Atlanta experience as a central component of the Gerontology in Theological Education (GITE) project.

How to Integrate Gerontology into Seminary Curriculum

Jim L. Waits, DD

SUMMARY. Dean Waits challenged the AGHE preconference session to integrate the theology of creation, covenant and care with the scientific findings in gerontology as important parts of the theological curriculum.

How do we integrate the concerns of the multidisciplinary field of gerontology into the multifaceted scope of a seminary curriculum? If our concern is truly to integrate gerontology into seminary education, then we will be cautious about a simple "add-a-course" approach. The whole theme will need to infuse our teaching and institutional priorities. Yet we need to steer clear of elaborate proposals to reorganize the curriculum as a whole. (The last thing we need is another reason to reorganize the curriculum!) How to bring the burgeoning field of gerontology to bear on the fiber of the seminary experience — that is what we all want to achieve from our varying perspectives. This common concern serves as our central focus.

Let us seek to do two things as we start our conversation. We will first of all draw on some central images from the Judeo-Christian faith that stand as foundational to our efforts. We will then move on to some preliminary reflections and, perhaps, models for institutional consideration. We will, in particular, look at some instances of institutional possibilities that have emerged and hopefully will be emerging out of our setting at Candler and Emory. These two components may be provocative enough to encourage a fruitful discussion.

Central to our self-understanding as religious persons is an

Jim L. Waits is Dean of the Candler School of Theology, Emory University.

5

awareness that we are part of God's creation. We affirm that all creation is the Lord's and that all persons are God's children, made in God's image. This affords an enormous respect to every human being and guarantees to him or her the dignity of a child of God. Where God's children are vulnerable, sick or deprived of the quality of life, we are called to serve. Because God created us, we are of immeasurable worth—and so are all those whom God made regardless of their weakness or current insufficiency.

This insistence on our ongoing participation in God's creation mitigates against our temptations to treat others and ourselves on the basis of some utilitarian ethic. It reminds us—lest we see life's meaning only in terms of a person's supposed usefulness or productivity—that our worth is God's to determine. And God created humanity, male and female. And behold it was very good. In our work with and for the elderly of our various communities, and in our views of ourselves, this image of creatureliness is essential. "Very good" we are called, irrespective of job title, income, disability, age, giftedness, or awareness.

Related to the central image of ourselves as creatures of God is the relational notion of ourselves in covenant. The image of covenant has been a constant in Old and New Testament times and throughout church history. God covenanted to be with us, to be a tangible presence among us, living with us, guiding and directing us. The covenant, though originally instituted by God with rare individuals like Noah, Abraham and Sarah, or Moses, was never individualistic in character. The covenant by its very nature was for God and the community, the people, the nation, the world. The covenant tied the people in faithfulness to their God, but also to one another with bonds deeper than blood, and priorities that ordered the fabric of day-to-day life.

The church has understood itself as a covenant community charged with the dual command to love God and love neighbor. It can never exist as a body of isolated individuals, but only with an intentional interdependency on one another. Only in community do we discover our individual giftedness and participate in giving and receiving as God's Spirit lives through us. In our encounters with persons who are aging, we all can see with new eyes our need for the perspectives of the old and the young. Just as we seek to love one another in community, in covenant, we have the happy experience of receiving from those to whom we would give. Over and over again our interdependency is proven as we relate across the generations.

But the affirmation most basic to our self-understanding is that we as religious people care. We love. Love, patterned after God's love, is the overriding motivation. In the circumstance of service and the never-ending frustrations and pressures of institutional life, we sometimes forget that singular value. But love (and care) must be the dominant motivation for all action and meaning-making. It is the clearest imperative for our service.

Love has many forms as it motivates us in ministry. It gives us eyes of insight and discernment. It gives us courage to live with or alongside the deepest human agony. It drives us to employ our faculties and energies against seemingly insurmountable odds.

Thus, we understand ourselves as instruments of God's creation, as a covenant community and as a people who are called to care. As we look at our task for this afternoon, then, these prior commitments stand before us to inform our question. How do we integrate gerontology into seminary curriculum? We begin by assessing and developing consensus about our motivation and theological rationale. But I would also like to recite some examples in our program as well as some future plans which we hope will advance this goal.

First of all, let us look at the curriculum, the course offerings that through a variety of perspectives and pedagogies address issues related to religion and aging. Since the mid-70s, Candler has offered a basic academic course on Religion and Aging, usually taught by Professor Earl Brewer, who is one of our leaders today. Out of this small beginning, a joint program with Georgia State University has developed so that our Master of Divinity students may receive a Certificate in Gerontology as well. In addition to the academic courses, set in the classrooms of Emory and Georgia State, students have also had the opportunity for more experiential learnings through our contextual program and supervised ministry. Second and third year students have had the option of participating in local congregations with large elderly populations or in institutions such as Wesley Woods and Northside Shepherd's Center. In such settings, the theological commitments — creation, covenant and care —

are brought into focus for the students as they experience an ongoing ministry with the elderly.

Some preliminary conclusions to our experiences with more traditionally academic settings and the contextual settings for students' learning have led us to believe that students need both. They need the rigors of sociological, psychological and theological disciplines in the classroom, but they also need the experiences of one-to-one ministries of care, the exposure to governmental bureaucracy as it affects the aging, and the congregational and community life that can so often sustain us at all ages. For our purposes, as we seek to integrate gerontology into the seminary curriculum, this is an important conclusion. We cannot, in other words, resort to simply adding a course here and there, or even a department, but must allow for an infusion of perspectives of gerontology across the curriculum. We have a commitment to both the academic and contextual learnings for students in the area of gerontology.

Another cluster of programs in which Candler has been involved has been cooperative ventures with other educational or institutional settings. The Georgia State University certification program is one example already mentioned. The Atlanta Theological Association, a consortium of seminaries, has offered joint courses with Georgia State University for MDiv and Doctor of Ministry students and for area ministers. We have also been particularly pleased that in our setting we have Wesley Woods, a residential center for the elderly, located only a few blocks away. For some years the Clinical Pastoral Education and Supervised Ministry programs have been in place there, offering experiences of one-to-one counseling, worship and community life. We have also had limited experience in internships which prepare persons for administrative roles in such institutions.

But there is a desire on the part of both institutions to develop more educational opportunities in such a setting. Our desires for further opportunities converge with the University's commitment to cooperate with Wesley Woods in staffing a major geriatric Medical Center adjacent to Wesley Woods. This center over time will provide care for thousands of people, as well as offer research and training opportunities for a number of disciplines. In theological education, our hope would be that the creation of such centers of intense care and learning might prompt us to create new understandings of our training of future ministers for the church. In such a center, theological education might include projects on topics such as the role of religious commitment to the aging process, demographic factors shaping our current and future communities and congregations, experiences in holistic health care inclusive of the spiritual dimension, and so on.

As we review the plethora of possibilities for research and teaching through such cooperative ventures, it is most encouraging. But to approach the many possibilities will take a commitment individually and institutionally. It will also require the best of our creative faculties to structure programs that include methods and content from the various disciplines within gerontology. Our focus, for example, cannot simply draw upon the discipline of psychology in setting up clinical experiences in pastoral care, but must also develop models of education that use the insights of social gerontology, social planning and policy studies, anthropology, cross-cultural studies of aging, and developmental studies. Bringing in such diverse fields will mean, as always in theological education, a continual dialogue or conversation with our theological tenets, and not wholesale adoption of methods without theological critique.

So in a sense we are brought full circle to the initial foundational claims with which we began — our commitment to the creation, to the covenant community and to care. These three in conversation with the methods, the insights, the research and the institutions of gerontology sketch out in broad strokes our agenda. It is time the community of theological institutions began to take seriously the dramatic developments in this field.

Three Seminaries and a Gerontology Center in Atlanta

Barbara Payne, PhD
Earl D. C. Brewer, PhD

SUMMARY. This section provides a description of Atlanta experience by the co-directors of the project. There is a brief history of the three seminaries and the gerontology center. Some responses of the students to the experience, a brief faculty survey and some suggestions for an introductory course complete this section.

The three seminaries (Candler School of Theology, Columbia Theological Seminary, Interdenominational Theological Center) and the Gerontology Center in Atlanta have worked together over a number of years to relate gerontology and theological education.

The Candler School of Theology is a professional school of Emory University and one of 13 official seminaries of the United Methodist Church. Candler serves to educate men and women for professional competence in ministry and the theological disciplines. Founded by the Methodist Episcopal Church, South, in 1914, the school became a part of Emory when the University was chartered in 1915. It occupied the first building completed on the Atlanta campus. The theology school offers programs leading to Master of Divinity, Master of Theological Studies, Master of Theology, Doctor of Ministry, and Doctor of Sacred Theology degrees. The school also provides continuing education opportunities for clergy, church professionals, and lay persons.

Columbia refers to the first permanent location of the seminary in

---

Barbara Payne is Director of the Gerontology Center of Georgia State University and Earl D. C. Brewer is Charles Howard Candler Professor Emeritus, Sociology and Religion, Candler School of Theology, Emory University.

Columbia, South Carolina, in 1828 a principal cultural, intellectual, and population center of the Southeast. The first idea of a theological school for the South was planted by the Presbytery of Hopewell (Georgia) as early as 1817, but it was not until 1824 that a constitution for "The Classical, Scientific, and Theological Institution of the South" was adopted by the Presbytery of South Carolina.

By the 1920s, the population of the Southeast—and of Presbyterians in the area—was shifting toward Atlanta and the centers of influence were moving with it. Certain Atlanta Presbyterians and leaders of the seminary were convinced of the city's leadership of the New South and its advantages for the seminary—and of the seminary for the city. In 1924, the Board of Directors agreed (after two previous refusals in 1887 and 1904), and the decision was made to move to Atlanta. In June, 1983 Columbia Theological Seminary became a seminary in the reunited Presbyterian Church (U.S.A.). Columbia Theological Seminary provides a community setting for theological education. In this context courses of study leading to both basic and advanced degrees are offered. The Master of Arts in Youth Ministry and the Master of Divinity are the first professional degrees. The Master of Arts in Theological Studies is also a basic theological degree, but academic rather than professional in orientation. Advanced degrees are the Master of Theology, the Doctor of Ministry (in ministry) and the Doctor of Sacred Theology.

Interdenominational Theological Center, was chartered in 1958 through the mutual efforts of four denominations, representing four schools of theology. The schools in order of their chronology are: (1) Morehouse School of Religion; (2) Gammon Theological Seminary; (3) Turner Theological Seminary and (4) Phillips School of Theology. Two other seminaries joined ITC later. They are (1) Johnson C. Smith Seminary and (2) Charles H. Mason Theological Seminary. Each of these seminaries has its own significant history. They bring together six denominations in ecumenical theological education. The Center offers five degree programs: Master of Divinity; Master of Arts in Religion; Master of Arts in Religion with concentration in Church Music; Doctor of Ministry; and Doctor of Sacred Theology. The Doctor of Sacred Theology and Doctor of Ministry degrees are offered in cooperation with other seminaries and agencies in the Atlanta Theological Association (ATA). The

MAR and MA degrees in Education are offered jointly with the School of Education of Atlanta University.

The Gerontology Center of Georgia State University is a university-wide organization that generates, coordinates and develops instruction, training, research and community service programs in the field of aging. Established in August, 1978 by the Board of Regents of the University System of Georgia, the Center is an outgrowth of the Department of Sociology's "Aging Studies Program," which had been engaged in training students for careers in gerontology since 1973. Faculty of the Center, drawn from 30 departments and administrative units representing the six colleges of the University, participate in instruction, research, consultation and technical assistance involving gerontological issues. Advisory to the Center is a Board of Counselors composed of representatives from community agencies, interested individuals and leaders in private industry. The Center offers specialized certificate programs of study in gerontology. Graduates of these programs have become leaders in the field of aging as administrators, educators, planners and practitioners in long-term care facilities, retirement communities, social service agencies, local and state planning agencies, church programs, mental health centers, home health agencies, and other facilities and programs offering services to older people.

The Gerontology Center and the three seminaries through the Atlanta Theological Association have carried out several joint programs. The first was a symposium on "Religion and Aging in Today's World" in 1978. The primary goal of this symposium was to explore the relationship between religion and the needs of the elderly in today's world. A secondary goal was to explore the place of gerontology in theological education and the role of the church in the field of aging.

In 1982, the second ATA-Center cooperative venture expanded to include, the Christian Council of Metropolitan Atlanta, the Presbyterian Office on Aging and the Georgia Department of Human Resources. It was a seminar on "Congregations and the Elderly." The purpose of the seminar was to develop cooperative models for congregations and agencies that meet the emerging needs of the elderly. Specific goals were developed by congregations and students during the seminar. The results of this seminar included the development of several coalitions of congregations in Atlanta around the needs and opportunities of older persons.

In 1985 a seminar on "Congregations and the Older Adult" was jointly offered. The purpose of the seminar was to explore ways congregations may meet the emerging needs of the elderly in their memberships and communities. This seminar was specifically designed for graduate students in gerontology and theology, pastors and lay persons from congregations, and staff members of agencies dealing with the elderly.

GERONTOLOGY IN THEOLOGICAL EDUCATION

In 1986-87, under a grant from Administration on Aging, the Gerontology Center and the three seminaries developed a two-term course on "Gerontology in Theological Education." The purpose of the fall term was to provide opportunities for seminary students to: (1) gain a basic understanding of the biological, psychological, and sociological approaches to the study of aging and their interrelationships; (2) to become familiar with the history, the concepts, and some of the basic literature of gerontology as a field of study; (3) to be able to read and critique social-scientific research that would enhance theological reflection and practices of ministry; (4) to be able to refine further their analytical skills in reading, understanding, conducting and applying research in gerontology to practices of ministries.

The topics included the biological and physiological aspects of aging, the psychology of aging and the social context of aging. There were appropriate subtopics under each of these. The faculty was composed of persons from Georgia State, Georgia Tech and Emory University with expertise in these areas of gerontology. They were: Delmas Allen, PhD, Biology; Angie Benham, PhD, Psychology; Charles Pyles, PhD, Political Science; Earl Brewer, PhD, Sociology; and Barbara Payne, PhD, Sociology.

In addition, a faculty member from each of the seminaries participated as postdoctoral fellows in gerontology: Nancy Ammerman, PhD, from Candler School of Theology; Edward Trimmer, EdD, from Columbia Theological Seminary; and Thomas Pugh, PhD, from the Interdenominational Theological Center.

During the spring term, the purpose was to become familiar with gerontological and theological principles and practices as they relate to ministries with, by and to the increasing numbers of older persons in congregations.

The topics dealt with various theological disciplines and practices. They included the following:

1. Liturgy, Worship and Older Persons
2. Faith Development and Older Persons
3. Theology and Older Persons
4. Church and Community and Older Persons
5. The Older Person within the Jewish Community
6. Congregational Programs and Older Persons
7. Church History and Older Persons
8. Bible and Older Persons
9. Pastoral Care and Older Persons
10. Spiritual Life and Older Persons
11. Preaching and Older Persons

Each topic had a presenter and a responding panel. There were 48 faculty members from the three seminaries involved in the process. Each was an expert in the topic being discussed. This provided a range of views and lively discussions by the panel and the students.

In addition to academic credit for this work, a special certificate in gerontology was available for each student. This involved the satisfactory completion of the two courses and additional work in field trips and placements in settings with older persons.

STUDENT RESPONSES

There were 22 students about equally divided from the three seminaries and four from Georgia State. Most of these participated in both fall and spring terms.

It is impossible to convey the richness and variety of the responses of the students to this experience. Getting in touch with one's own aging and developing a sensitivity to the needs of older persons in congregations and communities were often expressed. The growth in understanding of ministries to, with and through older persons was often expressed. What follows is a few of the written comments of students.

> We must be alert as helping professionals for sudden, perhaps pathological changes which are not part of the normal aging process, and recommend early medical treatment when it seems indicated.

> Hearing loss can be expected in older persons and we must be sensitive to the discomfort and possible social isolation it may cause. It is important that we be aware of elderly persons' vulnerabiliy to extremes of temperature, and advise on warm clothing in winter and overexertion in hot weather.

> While normal aging brings reduced interest and intensity of sexual response, it does not end sexual functioning. Helping professionals should take care in conversation to remember that identity is psychologically tied to sexual performance.

> As a minister, I will exercise caution when elderly parishioners ask me for medical or psychological advice. I will not try to be a physician or a psychologist but rather will listen and, if it seems warranted, refer them to the proper type of practitioner.

> As helping professionals, we can foster good health in our parishioners, particularly older adults by facilitating movement through the stages of grief as the stress associated with grief stimulates increased production of corticosteroid which suppresses the immune system, making people more susceptible to illness.

> Human touch may reduce blood pressure and stress. Keeping this in mind we can encourage appropriate intergenerational as well as peer touching to benefit elderly people who, in particular, tend to be more isolated from touch as well as other forms of interaction.

> My personal orientation has been present/future focused. I want to move to a more wholistic place, including the past in my focus. During the three months as I interviewed an 80-year-old woman, I have come to understand more fully the

mystery of life and to understand and, more importantly, to accept my own aging. For, I hope that as I age, I will be able to review and celebrate a rich and varied life: mourning the losses, reexperiencing many joys, and continuing to thank God for it all.

While there is a bit of sadness that comes with awareness of my own aging, I see myself as a worthwhile person of decent gifts and believe I can be useful to others and to the church in the coming years. I am well satisfied with the possibilities for a good life ahead.

As we age, in order to have the greatest possible chance for life satisfaction, we must have the freedom to choose which activities are maintained and which are discarded. Turning 50 and noticing physical change have made me aware of my own aging. While doors are closing on certain opportunities, new doors are opening to depth relationships and life satisfactions.

I'm becoming more and more interested in ministry to the elderly, finding myself anxious to learn of the needs of older Christians. I have come to an even deeper appreciation for the wisdom that comes from experience. In this way I can celebrate my own aging and what I gain in my daily experiences, although I dread the loneliness. We must distinguish between solitude and loneliness. Elders, like everyone else, need solitude to review and integrate their life experience. But if they lack an emotional support system, they may be lonely and loneliness is hazardous to both physical and psychological health.

As a minister I see myself playing more diverse roles as the proportion of older persons increases, and, particularly, I want to become attuned to the needs and problems of multigenerational families.

A question that has risen to the surface of my consciousness this quarter is, who will minister to the ministers as our callings become more diverse and complex, as we are called upon to deal with increasing numbers of elderly persons and their families?

With life expectancy increasing and the baby-boom generation nearing senior status, we must ensure that our churches keep pace by planning programming which will help increasing numbers of elders to find a place in society in which they feel they have something to offer.

I have become more aware that age stratification and prejudice against the elderly are part of our culture, even in church life. This seems more wrong to me than ever before and I want to have a part in changing it.

The church must consider the vast wealth it has in its older parishioners, efficiently utilizing their skills, experience and knowledge to improve the functioning of various ministries.

Ministry with elders needs a balance between the other-worldly and this-worldly; between the need for both doubt and faith; for the ministry of presence rather than platitudes.

An important, but often overlooked, area of ministry is discovering meaningful liturgies to provide rites of passage through the liminal times of aging.

I believe that it is very important that the aged be recognized as valuable members of the church. They provide an invaluable balance, helping us to see and proclaim the value of the wholeness of life and to remember that we are aging, too. I hope that as I become elderly the church will be there for me. Having deep roots in the congregation for support, death seems a much less fearful thing. A role ministers may play as the baby boomers become elderly persons will be to help the aging to enjoy meaningful later years while diffusing young adults' resentments.

Ministers must find ways to help lessen the stress of people in the middle years, who care for older parents as well as their own children and, perhaps, even grandchildren.

We must ask ourselves whether we will help society to segregate older adults into ghetto-like communities or facilitate intergenerational faith communities.

Aging-related political action groups, if they are to continue to be effective, must join with other social welfare interest groups on issues of great concern, such as national health insurance. I can think of few ways older people can have a greater sense of contributing to society than by becoming active in aging interest groups which are powerfully impacting public policy. Most aging-related public policy change has been initiated by white, middle/upper class people and organizations. I hope that in the future we will see more activity by and focus on elderly minorities in the public policy arena.

ATLANTA SEMINARY FACULTY RESPONSES TO GERONTOLOGY IN THEOLOGICAL EDUCATION

A brief questionnaire was mailed to 109 faculty members in the three seminaries: Candler School of Theology (53), Columbia Theological Seminary (29), and the Interdenominational Theological Center (27). Responses were received from 52 faculty members: Candler (22), Columbia (18) and ITC (12).

The 51 respondents were involved in the following curriculum areas: Ministry (15), Theology (12), Bible (9), History and Church and Society (5 each) and 5 in other areas.

Faculty members were asked to indicate the relation of their courses to aging (see Table 1).

It is clear from these responses that little attention is given to aging in the programs provided by these seminaries in the past and present. Several items dealt with the future of aging materials in the curriculum. These are shown with the mean scores which are based on a 1-4 scale. The higher the score the greater the agreement with the item (see Table 2).

There was strong agreement (Item 3) that there should be an elective course on aging but not a required course (Item 4). The faculty members felt that their seminary should cooperate with community agencies and centers of gerontology (Item 6) and sponsor research and teaching (Item 7). There was more support for Item 2 than Item 1.

TABLE 1

Relation of Courses	Percentage Answering "yes"
1. My courses are not related to aging issues	38.1
2. There are incidental references to aging in some of my courses	89.4
3. In one or more of my courses there are definite parts or modules dealing with aging	26.2
4. I teach a separate course on the relation of my area of work to aging...........................	10.0
5. I participate in a team-taught course on aging.....	2.6
6. I participate in field education work related to the elderly.......................................	26.8

Item 8 had to do with the importance of faculty members getting in touch with their own aging. There was almost unanimous agreement with this idea. This is interesting in view of the ages of the faculty. Nearly two-thirds were under 55 years with a fourth between 55 and 65 and a tenth 65 and over.

A short quiz was given to the faculty members. The true-false items are shown in Table 3 with the percent of correct responses by the faculty.

The majority of the faculty members gave the correct answers on all items except Items 3 and 5. In Item 3, they did not know their statistics. In 1980 those 65 and over made up 11.3 percent of the total population of the United States. It is projected to become 13.0 percent by 2000.

Only 40.4 percent knew that Item 5 was false. While it might seem reasonable to assume that older persons tend to become more religious as they age, evidence from various studies does not support that idea. The facts seem to indicate that people relate to religion in older years in about the same ways as in younger years.

This questionnaire was only a small part of the program introducing gerontology to students and faculties in these three seminaries. The findings indicate that not much is currently being done in this field. Yet the need for gerontology in theological education was

TABLE 2

Item	Score
1. Ministry is for all ages and no special attention should be given to any particular age group	2.1
2. The implications for older adults should be drawn out and discussed in all courses	2.6
3. There should be an elective course dealing with older adults	3.6
4. There should be a required course dealing with older adults	1.9
5. There should be aspects or modules dealing with older adults in all appropriate courses	3.1
6. Our seminary should cooperate with community agencies and centers of gerontology in its education for ministries with the elderly	3.5
7. Our seminary should sponsor research and teaching in the field of congregations and aging	3.2
8. It is important that faculty members be in touch with their own aging	3.5

recognized. Plans to do something about this were expressed in answers to the questions and in meetings with faculty members.

SUGGESTIONS FOR AN INTRODUCTORY COURSE

This project included a two semester introductory course involving gerontology for seminary students. The purpose here is to reflect on the Atlanta experience and to suggest key elements in an introductory course. It is hoped that these proposals may be helpful to faculty developing new introductory courses in this field as well as to those evaluating existing courses. Such introductory courses may cover one or two semesters. The material may also be useful in modules for a variety of seminary courses.

There is a confluence of two streams of knowledge and practice in these proposals. The first concerns the scientific knowledge of the aging process and the needs of older persons. The second deals with the relationships of the elderly to theological disciplines and

TABLE 3

Item	Percentage of Correct Responses
1. Most old people have no interest in, or capacity for, sexual relations	96.2
2. Aged drivers have fewer accidents per person than drivers under age 65	69.2
3. Over 15% of the U.S. population are now 65 or over	5.8
4. Older workers have fewer accidents than younger workers	82.7
5. Older people tend to become more religious as they age	40.4
6. About 80% of the aged are healthy enough to carry out their normal activities	84.6

clergy practices. The adequacy of the interflow of these will be a measure of the success of these suggestions.

During the presentations of the gerontological material it would be helpful to have a theological respondent. Likewise, a gerontological respondent might be on hand during the theological presentations. Even if this is not possible, the implications of these two streams for each other and for the future of older persons should be discussed.

A relational model is utilized as an organizing principle for the course. The older person is viewed as involved in four basic sets of relationships: (1) physical relationships including the body and the physical environment; (2) personal relationships including self-image and the psychic environment; (3) social relationships including the informal and formal social environments; and (4) spiritual relationships including conceptions and involvements with ultimate concerns and entities. The latter becomes a bridge between gerontological and theological material.

The themes or topics may be developed in keeping with the curriculum style of the seminary. They may include lectures, panels, discussions, field visits and other appropriate teaching-learning approaches. The units deal with suggested curriculum content, leaving the methods to the uniqueness of the instructor and the seminary. Some units may require more than one class session.

Items starred in the annotated bibliography in the companion volume may be especially useful in an introductory course or in special modules.

Unit 1. Introduction and Orientation

The goal is to introduce the course and orient students to its scope, purposes, requirements, style, bibliography, assignments and its place in the curriculum of the seminary. Obviously, this will be unique to each teacher and seminary as will be the specific design and content of the course.

Orientation to the older population involves a review and interpretation of the significant demographic facts and trends. This may include a discussion of the importance of cohorts, aging and period effects. Examples are the depression and baby boomers cohorts.

Unit 2. Physical Relations of Older Persons

The goal is to explore the impact of the aging process on the physical body and its physical environment.

Material is drawn from the biological sciences or physical gerontology and abnormal development in the bodies of older persons. Such would cover the skin, the nervous system, brain, the urinary system, and sensory system, skeletal system, muscles, and female reproductive system. It is important for clergy to understand the outward signs of normal and abnormal aging in these various systems of the body and to counsel persons where appropriate and to make referrals to geriatric physicians.

The second concern of the physical aspects of aging has to do with the changing relationship of the older person's body to its physical environment. While the various physical sciences may contribute here, the focus is on human ecology and the planning of environments. Such elementary things as the purity of air and water, the choice and availability of foods, housing options, barrier-free buildings, available transportation, safety and convenience, and the beauty of surroundings could be reviewed.

The role of clergy in planning for more adequate and pleasing environments for the elderly should be explored. The ethical implications of inadequate resources, bad housing (in their own homes or in nursing homes), poor diets, often limited medical care and the ethics of the right to die and to live should be explored. The implications for clergy practice and congregational programs for the adequacy of physical environments of older persons are enormous.

Unit 3. Personal Relations of Older Persons

The goal of this unit is to explore the personal relations of the elderly. The focus is on the psychological aspects of gerontology and clergy counseling of older persons. A faculty member in counseling and a psychologist with specialization in gerontology would make an ideal teaching team. Topics to be covered include self-image, life review and preview, relationships to significant others such as family members, intergenerational relations and close friends, personal problems of the elderly such as a sense of loss, Alzheimer's disease, psychological impairment, and coping with issues of death and dying. The role of clergy in counseling and the congregational care for older impaired persons should be stressed. Also, opportunities for the continued involvement of active older adults in the ministries of the congregation should be provided. This is probably the greatest gift of clergy and congregations to older persons.

Unit 4. Social Relations of Older Persons

The goal of this unit is to explore the relations of older persons in the society, community, and congregation. Experts in the various aspects of social gerontology and in clergy practices in congregation and community would make suitable teams for presenting this unit.

The unit covers a wide range of topics and is related to the demographics material covered in Unit 1.

1. Older persons and family/intergenerational relations
2. Older persons and continued educational opportunities
3. Older persons and governmental/political relationships
4. Older persons and artistic/recreational relationships

5. Older persons and religious/congregational relationships
6. Older persons and health/welfare relationships
7. Older persons and economic relationships (as consumers, in the work force, poverty, etc.)

Unit 5. Spiritual Relations of Older Persons

The goal of this unit is to explore the spiritual relations of older persons. This theme becomes a bridge between gerontological material and theological disciplines and practices.

There should be a review of the literature on spiritual well-being of older persons. Note the paucity of material on this topic. Each seminary and congregation will have its own beliefs and practices regarding the spiritual life. Several of the presentations in the Atlanta experience contain appropriate material.

Unit 6. The Relation of Theological Disciplines to Older Persons

The goal of this unit is to explore the concerns for older persons in the various disciplines of theological education. The papers presented in the Atlanta experience will be useful. Faculty with expertise in these several disciplines could be invited to make presentations. Also, it might be stressed that modules on the involvement of older adults would be appropriate in courses dealing with these disciplines. This introductory course could hardly afford more than one or two sessions for each discipline. Each seminary will have its own way of identifying its theological disciplines. Here is one way of doing it.

1. Bible and Older Persons
2. History, Tradition and Older Persons
3. Theology/Ethics and Older Persons
4. Religions Education/Faith Development and Older Persons
5. World Religions and Older Persons
6. Psychology of Religion and Older Persons
7. Sociology of Religion and Older Persons

Unit 7. The Relation of Clergy Practices
to Older Persons

The goal of this unit is to review the major practices expected of clergy and relate them to the needs of older persons in congregations and communities.

The appropriate papers from the Atlanta experience should be helpful. It may be necessary to use more than one session on some of these practices. The involvement of experts in these fields is encouraged. Also, teachers should be challenged to include the needs and opportunities of older persons in their regular courses. This list of practices may be modified to fit into the tradition of each seminary.

1. Pastoral Counseling and Older Persons
2. Preaching (speech, hearing, communications) and Older Persons
3. Worship/Music/Liturgy and Older Persons
4. Congregational Programs and Older Persons
5. Community Outreach and Older Persons

Obviously, teaching plans for an introductory course or for modules in other courses could be developed in various ways. These suggestions emerge from the Atlanta experience and may be helpful to others.

Gerontology in the Three Atlanta Seminaries: Views of the Post-Doctoral Fellows

Nancy T. Ammerman, PhD
Edward A. Trimmer, EdD
Thomas Pugh, PhD

SUMMARY. These three faculty members were involved in the program throughout the year. Among other responsibilities, they prepared reports on the possibilities of integrating concerns for the elderly into the curricula of their seminaries. These reports were shared with the faculties of their seminaries. In a somewhat shortened form, their reports follow.

CANDLER SCHOOL OF THEOLOGY: NANCY T. AMMERMAN

The year-long program on gerontology in theological education led to the conviction that a two-fold approach to issues of aging is needed in theological education.

First, all faculty members need to become more aware of those issues and the theological/ministry challenges they raise, thereby integrating an awareness of and concern for older people into all aspects of our teaching. This kind of consciousness-raising is not unlike what we have experienced as we have come to terms with other issues of inclusiveness.

Nancy T. Ammerman is Professor of Sociology of Religion, Candler School of Theology, Emory University. Edward A. Trimmer is Professor of Christian Education, Columbia Theological Seminary. Thomas Pugh is Professor of Pastoral Care, Interdenominational Theological Center.

Second, specialized courses, units within courses, and field placements are also needed. Students need to understand the nature of the aging process and the place of older adults in church and society.

The rest of this report to the faculty is an effort to begin both those tasks. Let me invite you to read and file the report in its entirety for use in thinking about your own teaching and your advising of students. To catch the most relevant highlights, look over the "consciousness-raising" section and then turn directly to the material for your area of the curriculum.

Consciousness-Raising: What Is the Issue?

There are more people over 65 today than ever before, and they form a larger percentage of the population, as well. That is, people are living longer and the birth rate is declining. These basic demographic facts create major economic and political changes, suggest shifts in culture and life patterns, and generally call into question basic expectations about the nature and meaning of work, family, and health.

In the churches the picture is even more dramatic. Because the generation now 30-45 has shunned the church in large numbers, the decline on the younger end accentuates further the increasing percentage of older members. In the North Georgia Conference of the United Methodist Church, for instance, 17.2% of the members are over 65 (compared to 9.5% of the state's population), with an additional 15.2% aged 55-64.

The existence of this large block of older church members raises a variety of issues for pastoral ministry and for theology more generally, but before we can address those issues we must better understand who these members are and some helpful distinctions.

"Young-Old" and "Old-Old"

As early as age 55 many Americans have entered some aspects of the "elderly" role — grandparenting, career transitions, perhaps early retirement, and so forth. They are entering a stage of life experienced by relatively few in earlier generations where "retirement" was unknown and fathers on average died before the last child reached maturity. However, the average person in this "young-old" category today can expect to live at least 20 more years, is probably in good health, and may have adequate financial resources. They often have increased discretionary time and need minimal social services. The "young-old" do have needs, but they may not be the needs people usually associate with being "elderly."

The truly elderly, the "old-old," are those often over 75, faced with significant loss of physical capacity. They may still live for several years, but require higher levels of care. Here needs include advocacy for the well-being and dignity of the person, continued involvement in networks of interaction, and care for the care-givers, especially family members dealing with this new kind of dependency.

Aging, Period, or Cohort Effects

People don't get more religious just because they are getting older. That would be an "aging" effect. Today's generation of elders was brought up in a more "religious" time and has carried that upbringing with it through the years. This involves both "cohort" and "period" effects. It remains to be seen what will happen to "baby boomers" when they are 65 but don't expect them to return to church just because they have gotten old!

"Ministry To" and "Ministry With"

Older adults certainly have needs worth caring about and to which ministry ought to be addressed. However, a theology of persons and churches that takes lay vocations seriously will not cease to value the ministry of a person because that person has diminished physical capacities or has passed "retirement age." Among the challenges presented by a large group of older adults is the challenge of rethinking the nature of vocation, discipleship, and ministry.

A sample of other basic theological/ministry questions:

What does it mean to live a significant portion of one's life "free" of work and family obligations? How do we think about human "value" in cases of prolonged and significant incapacity? What are the responsibilities of younger people (and the society as a whole) in relation to their elders? What is the role of the "elder" in the community of faith? What special gifts can older members bring to the work and worship of the church? And, of course, how do we integrate the realities of limits, decline, and death into our understanding of human life?

The final section of this report offers a more detailed outline of relevant issues and resources for each area of the Candler curriculum.

Area I: Biblical Studies

Issues: Gerontological issues seem to bear most on the treatment of basic biblical "anthropology." What view is presented in the biblical record of the nature of long life and of the human vocation? What scriptural resources may address issues of work, family obligations, health, and so forth?

Current offerings: None of the Atlanta seminaries offers a specific course focussing on issues of aging in scripture.

Area II: History and Interpretation of Christianity

Issues in Theology: In his presentation to the Gerontology class, Professor Runyon pointed out that folk religion (including hymnody) has seen old age as a time to get one's house in order, to get ready for heaven. However, that may be an increasingly uncommon way to experience aging. Just as the life span is extending dramatically, many educated folk are doubting the reality of heaven as an ultimate reward. Belief in an afterlife can either rob the older person's life of meaning or lend meaning to it. Meaning may be gained when all of life, including aging, is seen as a pilgrimage and when hope is anchored in a vision of the kingdom coming to meet us. He, and others, raised theological questions about the meaning of vocation and leisure, hope in this life and hope in life beyond, grace and works, and so forth.

Issues in Church History: In her presentation, Professor Gonzalez (of Columbia) pointed out that the church's understanding of aging and death has changed as the realities of life and death have changed. The church's relationship to older people (especially widows) was usually one of charity but has also had elements of exploitation in it. Professor Pacini pointed out that the very absence of attention to the problems of aging in the history of the church represents a kind of relegation of a disadvantaged population to nonexistence. However, in many other traditions (notably African ones) elders have had some status based on their links to the oral history and wisdom of the community. But in the last two centuries in the Western world, rapid change has made such status based on age less likely. These issues raised questions about precedents, both good and bad, offered us by the history of the church.

Current Offerings: None of the Atlanta seminaries currently offers coursework focussed on the historical place of "elders" or on the theological issues of long life, aging, and/or death.

Area III: Christianity and Culture

Issues in Religion and Personality: Professor Gerkin outlined several hermeneutical models of aging. The most dominant is a model in which aging is characterized by "anguish" at the diminishment of both capacity and remaining life. Other psychological models emphasize loss/compensation and/or epigenetic sequences. A more theologically grounded model rests on an eschatology of hope which takes seriously both the limitations experienced in aging and a vision of God's future for both person and creation.

Professor Fowler noted that elders may be at various faith stages, and those stages may affect how they respond to their own aging. Those at Stage 2 may lack the interiority and self-perspective to be able to understand their own aging process. Those at Stage 3 may so completely define themselves in terms of relationships that retirement and death are especially fearful. Those at Stage 4 may think of themselves as free individuals and be unsettled by the dependencies of age.

Additional issues include adequate attention to the cognitive processes of aging and to explanations of development that do not assume greater religiosity with age.

Issues in Sociology of Religion: Throughout the year themes of both exclusion and change dominated our discussion. Elders are systematically excluded from structures of involvement and power both in American society and in churches. On the other hand, the existence of this new stage in the life cycle is calling forth social change and innovation.

Issues in Ethics: All the issues of economic and social justice are relevant to the aging. In addition, long life raises special questions in medical ethics.

Current Offerings at Candler: SPE301, Society and Personality (required course), contains some attention to issues of both psychology and sociology of aging; SR311, Religion and Aging (elective, offered every three years), treats issues of aging in church and community; RP335, Adult Development and Aging (elective), uses developmental models to examine the aging process and implications for ministry.

At Emory: SOC550, Socialization, Society and the Life Cycle (graduate level); SOC348, Aging in Society (undergraduate); various courses in developmental psychology (graduate and undergraduate).

Area IV: Church and Ministry

Issues in Preaching and Worship: Professor Craddock reminded us that a good preacher "exegetes" the congregation (and that includes all ages), uncovering the life experiences that shape how they hear preaching. He urged preachers to be truly inclusive, being as sensitive to "little old lady" jokes as to derogatory remarks about other disadvantaged or minority groups. In addition, illustrations should be inclusive of old as well as young. He especially noted that what ultimately binds old and young together is scripture and tradition. What elders especially need to hear (and the rest, too) is the value of life apart from productivity (a true theology of grace). They also need an opportunity to embrace what cannot be changed, especially death, a subject too often taboo in the pulpit. Finally, elders need challenge to continue to grow in the life of discipleship.

Professor Melba Costen (of ITC) noted several dimensions of worship that involve the encounter of finite humans with the infinity and mystery of God. The presence of aging persons may remind all of us of those dimensions of finitude. Costen emphasized the need for worship to be the work of the people, reflecting their lives. And Professor Ward encouraged making space for the telling of stories so that all may hear the dimensions of life experience elders have to offer the congregation. Costen also noted the need for all the senses to be involved, including touch.

Issues in Christian Education: Pastor/teachers need to know the facts about adult learning before they proceed to make assumptions about how to teach (or not teach) older persons.

Issues in Pastoral Care: There are a number of ways in which sustaining is called for, but so are guiding, healing, and reconciling. The pastoral theological model Professor Gerkin developed has clear implications for giving and receiving of care.

Issues in Church and Community: The church is often a "frontline" agency in connecting older persons with needed services and can often help to translate these personal "troubles" into the political issues underlying them.

Current Offerings at Candler: Pastoral Care of Aging Persons and their Families (offered periodically by adjunct faculty for 1 credit hour).

Contextual Education at Candler is involved with the elderly. Current offerings include Supervised Ministry I, Wesley Woods; Supervised Ministry II, DeKalb Community Council on Aging, Northside Shepherd Center. Additional settings including some work with elders are Atlanta Public Housing, Project: Rescue, Atlanta Emergency Aid Ministry, Christian Council of Metropolitan Atlanta. Ministry Internships include Pacesetters (Macon District Ministry for Older Adults), Decatur Cooperative Ministry (FISH service), Wesley Woods.

COLUMBIA THEOLOGICAL SEMINARY: EDWARD A. TRIMMER

There appear to be at least two avenues by which one might seek to bring gerontology and gerontological concerns to theological institutions. One would be by adding classes either elective or required. The other would be integrating gerontological concerns in existing classes either elective or required.

Before this project there were only three courses in the curriculum which addressed gerontology issues and no classes that integrated gerontological concerns into existing classes. The three classes that were already present were: Adult Education in the Congregation—a Christian Education elective offered every two years that rarely did anything specifically with gerontology; Clinical Pastoral Education (CPE)—a highly specialized pastoral care course with placement available at Wesley Woods, a United Methodist retirement home; and Pastoral Care and Aging Process. This latter course while listed in the catalogue had not been taught since its design and initial offering as part of the GIST project.

This project has allowed a Christian Education faculty member to be educated in the area of gerontology and to offer a specific course, Christian Education with Older Adults. This course has been added to the elective offerings available in the pastoral area and is scheduled to be taught every two years. This course would normally attract students from the MDiv, DMin, and ThM degree programs.

This project has also aroused some awareness to the issue of gerontology and the implications for ministry. Thus, the pastoral care faculty are going to offer Pastoral Care and the Aging Process, and a gerontology placement for the introductory course in pastoral care has been put in place. Additionally, we have discovered some DMin students who will continue to focus on gerontology in their DMin course and project designs. Unfortunately, despite the heightened awareness, both the Biblical and Historical/Doctrinal areas are not ready to integrate gerontological concerns into their courses or add new courses.

Master of Divinity
(Wayne Morrison Contributed
to This Segment)

Since over 78% of the courses in the MDiv degree program are required, it may be more appropriate to discuss the integration of gerontological concerns into existing courses. Any additional required courses will meet with tremendous opposition. Further, there is a theoretical concern that may be expressed in this manner when examining the integration of gerontology into existing courses: why should gerontological concerns take precedence over child issues, youth issues, handicapped issues, single issues or any other issue? To be wholistic and to provide an appropriate theological education for the entire human life span, gerontology ought not to take priority over the other areas. However, it ought to be emphasized and lifted up as are the other areas of the human life span. Thus, the basic introductory course to the Practical Theology area, Becoming a Minister to Persons, will now include some human development in the later years as will the basic introductory course on Christian Education, The Ministry of Teaching. Further, the basic introductory course on pastoral care, Ministry to Persons, has recently added a gerontological field placement opportunity.

If for no other reason than a statistical mandate, all seminaries must look seriously at addressing gerontological issues. Simply stated, in twenty years there will be a lot of older people in the church. By the year 2000 more than 35 million citizens of the United States will be over the age of 65. As the baby boomers continue to mature, and the average life expectancy continues to rise, the biggest bulge in the populations age breakdown will be those over 65 years of age. Thus, from a purely physical standpoint, the church should be preparing to accommodate an aging population.

However, the biggest challenge to the church and seminaries is to address the aging process theologically so that educational programming for older adults will: (1) Help reshape social attitudes toward the aging, (2) Help redirect social trends involving the elderly, (3) Help to provide for the continuing spiritual development of older adults, and (4) Help to permeate the entire congregation and community with a reverence for the aged and the aging process of life.

When looking at the current MDiv program it is difficult to see how any new hours could be added regarding gerontological concerns. There could always be another elective added here or there, but somehow the concerns of the elderly in and out of the church need to be addressed within the required curriculum so that the entire student body will have at least some exposure to the needs of what will be one of the largest groups in the church.

There is no way that the MDiv program could stand an additional requirement without eliminating an equal number of hours from another area. Realizing how jealously each department guards its time, some suggestions can be made within the existing framework.

If the faculty made an intentional effort to be aware of and include gerontological concerns within their departments, all of the courses as they stand could keep these issues in front of the students. I'm thinking here of something similar to the way the issue of inclusive language was addressed within the curriculum. For all its controversy, there has been an elevating of student consciousness regarding the issue, largely as a result of the faculty's concern. If the faculty would spend the same energy in the area of gerontology, I believe the result would be the same.

More specifically, in the Junior Year (first year) Becoming A Minister to Persons, more time could be spent on the eighth and final stage of Erik Erikson's development schema. Perhaps the students could write a brief essay on an additional ninth stage. Further, the Ministry of Teaching course focus can be sharpened, not necessarily on specific teaching techniques but on the emotional and physical world of the elderly: life maintenance needs, life enrichment needs, life reconstruction needs, life transcendent needs. Additionally during Worship and Preaching one class session might be devoted to preaching and worship to the elderly.

In the Middler year (second year), Reformed Theology could expand the time spent on the Doctrine of Human Beings and deal directly with the theological aspects of value, purpose and calling. The aging of our population demands that we take a second look at questions concerning calling and vocation.

What appears to be the most natural area in which to expand gerontological issues is in the senior year/Spring component of Church and Ministry. As the course stands now, there is too much material to be covered in one semester but not enough to fill up two. By including and expanding the church's ministry to older adults, it would help to remedy an awkward situation in the curriculum.

In addition, each student could be required once or twice each year to worship at one of the area retirement homes or shepherd centers. There could be any number of chapel services designated to addressing these concerns, and special forums with guests representing various segments of Atlanta's aging population, in or out of the church.

To conclude, the base from which to address gerontological concerns is already present within the existing curriculum. With an intentional effort on the faculty's part, the raising of consciousness regarding these issues would be accomplished. In addition, these issues should be brought into the Spring section of the Church and Ministry course. The thrust of the educational effort needs to remain the raising of student consciousness and sensitivity. The elderly know what they need better than we do, and the first thing they need is a church community that is aware of them, sensitive to them, appreciative of their gifts, and willing to listen to them. Not only so the elderly can be ministered to but, more importantly, so the church can receive the ministry the elderly have to offer.

Master of Arts in Youth Ministry (Catherine Allsbury Contributed to This Segment)

The M.A.Y.M. program is focused on issues of adolescence in the American cultural context. Young persons do not exist in a vacuum, however, but in a faith community that usually includes several generations. A way to deal with gerontological issues in this degree program is to explore intergenerational activities. This type of church programming could be touched on in several of the required courses. Most church curriculum is age graded; most program ideas assume age segregation. The practice is so widespread that it is nearly a sacred law in many church schools. It would be helpful to examine alternatives to this approach. Intergenerational curriculum could be examined in the (basic) Christian Education course, as well as the standard age-graded material. Some brainstorming about intergenerational programs and projects could be done in either The Child and the Church course or one of the Youth Ministry classes. Looking at intergenerational programming could be included in case studies in the course on Educational Program and Leadership Development. Such lessons would do some consciousness-raising about possibilities for intergenerational activities.

A short unit on educating young people about aging, perhaps as an optional project in Advanced Youth Ministry is another possibility. Children and youth groups are frequently asked to visit in convalescent homes at Christmas. However, these young people, and often their advisors as well, are not prepared to deal with the frail and failing people they encounter on these good-will tours. Certainly this study might also foster greater understanding between young people and their elderly relatives.

Some exposure to gerontological concerns will now occur as these students take required courses such as Ministry of Teaching. However, addressing gerontology as an issue in interacting with the faith community would be appropriate.

Master of Theology
(Carol Abrams Contributed
to This Segment)

The Master of Theology (ThM) program at Columbia Theological Seminary is an advanced degree program beyond the MDiv. A student may concentrate his or her studies in one of the following fields: Biblical studies, historical-doctrinal studies, pastoral studies or pastoral counseling. Each degree requires 24 semester hours of academic work, including a minimum of 12 credits in the area of concentration and at least 6 credits in one of the other areas. A practicum is also required for the degree in pastoral counseling. All students is the ThM program are required to write a thesis.

It would be possible to include a specialized study of gerontological issues into any of the above areas of concentration. A student would be able to take the Gerontology and Theological Education program as offered through the seminary and Georgia State and still be able to complete the required credits in the area of concentration. The thesis could then focus on a particular issue of aging within that academic area.

Doctor of Ministry
(Chris Zorn and Rupert A. Young
Contributed to This Segment)

The Doctor of Ministry (In-Ministry) program at Columbia Seminary is established in cooperation with the Atlanta Theological Association. With over two hundred ministers currently enrolled, it is by far the largest program among the four participating seminaries. About 80% of those enrolled are parish ministers. There is an increasing interest in the area of aging and ministry, especially from pastors in Florida.

The DMin program has four components: (1) a core seminar, 6 hours; (2) supervised ministry, 6 hours; (3) electives, 18 hours; and (4) a doctoral project, 6 hours.

The core seminar is designed to look at all aspects of ministry. It seeks to help the student assess his or her own ministry style and interests. Core seminars are taught in Atlanta each fall, by a joint ATA faculty. The core is also taught for Columbia students in satellite locations. The time devoted to developmental issues is one-half of a day. The model used is that of Daniel Levinson. This is the only opportunity for aging concerns to be addressed, unless a particular student has special concerns regarding his or her ministry setting.

Two or three students have done supervised ministry in a home for the aging. However, the seminary is receptive to qualified locations in aging settings.

Electives are not usually offered in age-specific topics. This summer there will be a departure as Columbia offers its first DMin elective in Aging to be taught by Dr. Al Dimmock. Students are allowed to transfer up to 6 hours into the DMin program. Thus, it is conceivable that graduate courses in gerontology could be taken at state schools, or the Presbyterian School of Christian Education and credited to a program at Columbia. Also, four hours may be taken through independent studies. It is possible that a student could take two 2-hour reading courses in aging concerns.

Here are two examples of doctoral projects in the area of Religion and Aging:

— Sara Miriam Dunson, "Pastoral Care with Older Adults Through the Psalms," 1985.
— Robert Floyd Inman, "Lay Ministry with the Elderly Shut-Ins," 1985.

One development is that for about three years one of the satellite core courses has been taught at the Presbyterian Home, Inc. at Summerville, South Carolina. Ministers interact with the older adult residents. This has been a mutually rewarding venture.

There are points to introduce pertinent gerontological data and there is a role for the seminary to carry out in advocacy. During the core course it would be appropriate to discuss the demographic facts about aging and the dramatic increase of older adults predicted for the next thirty years. Ministers need to reflect upon the impact that increasing numbers of elderly and increasing life spans will have upon the culture in general and upon the church in particular. A minister trained at a doctoral level should be expected to have dealt with personal fears of aging and death, as well as unexamined biases toward and stereotypes of older adults.

The educating of persons on the faculty with skill and resources in gerontology will provide more and more opportunity for doctoral students to consider this area of study. In addition, the seminary should act as an advocate for the concerns of the elderly.

INTERDENOMINATIONAL THEOLOGICAL CENTER: THOMAS PUGH

On taking my pen in hand after positioning myself at the desk with the intention being to tell a story of a year's experience in school studying gerontology, my memory was stimulated. I could not make a record of all of the matters that appeared there because of the differences in tempo that my pen could move and the tempo with which my thoughts were registered into consciousness. It becomes a year in retrospect. But the fact of the matter is that more shall be recorded here than happened in that year. This is due to how what happened during that time period, as in a dream, brought things from the long ago to a level of consciousness that had been forgotten.

In Virginia, one summer during my high school years, one day visiting a couple who had migrated there from back home, the wife introduced me to Emiline who lived next door. She was a little lady who rode the streetcar to work regularly three days a week. She masticated food on her gums, followed a diet of lamb, fish and vegetables, attended church regularly and took care of Albert, a nephew, about half her age. He was an asthmatic who drank heavily and fussed at Emiline when he had been drinking. He would not work. Emiline was eighty-six years of age. I thought it was terrible. Since that time I have learned a good deal about the nature of human nature from psychology, the social and physical sciences, and history. This case contradicts the belief of some people regarding the elderly.

Gerontology in Theological Education was a systematic study of aging with an equal number of students from three seminaries and the university that hosted the study—Georgia State. The typical pattern in the study of gerontology puts emphasis on three major elements—biological, psychological and social. This we sought to amend. Depending upon need, the major elements are supplemented with economics, social work and medicine. In the study in which we were engaged, a considerable amount of time was given to the major elements as foundation for an equal amount of time to the theological elements: Liturgy, Worship, Faith Development, Theology, Church and Community, Church History, Bible, Pastoral Care, Spiritual Life and Preaching. These were necessary also to serving the deeper internal needs of the elderly.

Gerontology is in a period of growth and development and, as such, commands attention in many disciplines. It will maintain this posture until it develops sufficiently to stand alone—which may not be far into the future. There can be interdependence of disciplines for the study until that time. Psychology had a similar evolutionary development, and marriage and family therapy even more so. Rapid growth in the older population and research therein will speed up change toward independence. Until that time comes, attention will be given the subject by persons who are informed and curious and act in a research posture to find more about this stage of life. If the life cycle is divided into three parts: beginning, middle and end, as Pruyser suggests, the second and third parts are movable continually with changes in longevity. The following is a digest of some ideas born during this study time.

Aging is a lifetime process. Life of a human being begins at a size that is very small. The signs of growth and development are continuous to adulthood. If this is the beginning stage, the first twenty years are likely to remain nearly constant. The person is constantly changing till death and beyond. Everyone is aging as long as s/he lives, and chronologically is getting older continually.

Social-human relationships are intergenerational. In the parent-child relationship there is a minimum of two generations. Depending upon where one is, there may be more than two generations living close to each other even if they do not share space under the same roof. In the intergenerational factors in human relations we can point to similarities and differences. The basic needs of the members of the generations are the same. But there are interests important to the particular generation that makes them different. The good of all may be better served with cooperation between and/ or among them.

Folks advancing in age present a picture of the normal curve of distribution. The needs of people even in old age vary with the individual. This is so despite the physical changes and the increased possibility of being susceptible to illnesses, disease and accident. Strengths, skills and interests are as evident as at the other stages of life. It is not a time for categorical disengagement of life.

Old age is especially suited to theological reflection. The explorations at this stage are as constant as the need to explore in the beginning stage. Experiences of losses and seeking spiritual help to understand and adapt to these make demands because of their frequency and closeness. There seems to be something in this stage that makes generosity a dominant trait. Does it mean that this is where learning and experience have brought persons in the height of their wisdom? That there is acceptance of the ultimate: "We brought nothing into the world, and it is certain we shall carry nothing out." Or is it an awareness of, at least, accepting the fact that no less will be required of the creature than of the Creator as demonstrated by his Son?

The question raised by the above is, what has this led to? A fact of life is that there tends to be more old people in church than in the general population. Several faculty persons from the seminaries and Georgia State had glimpses of the study and shared them. Time will help us understand what sort of follow-up ought to be in continuous course offering and how to get it programmed.

ITC's Summer School offered, for the first time, a course in gerontology called "Ministry, Theology and Gerontology." It is listed in the catalog under Pastoral Care. There has not been any attention given to the matter as a faculty for its ongoing. This, however, does not mean that persons from other disciplines in the faculty can not or will not be utilized for interdisciplinary input and information in this study. My concern is that it be given proper attention in all of the information structures for learning—the seminary curriculum, continuing education and workshops in churches. It has taken a long time, in America, to provide for the inclusion of gerontology in the various disciplines and ministries because the percentage of the population has not been large enough to deem it important. This has been changing. The emphasis found in some universities before now which said, "It offers education for learning from the cradle to the grave," did not include knowledge of the elderly as the Arnold Lucius Gesell longitudinal studies included knowledge of the developing person toward adulthood.

The course in gerontology in theological education provided a model for cooperation in theological education that I perceived as profitable. Cooperation makes for more success and personal gratification than does competition, which tends toward isolation and negativisms. In the cooperative context, winners and losers are not required or necessary—everybody wins. This may be a goal of the Atlanta Theological Association (ATA). What is seen here points toward the direction to become more intentional about this. On this becoming the growing edge of ATA, it could provide guidance for the Association of Theological Schools and thus the American commonwealth. Cooperation has possibilities for far-reaching positive effects.

How can Georgia State continue what it has begun? Having offered "Gerontology in Theological Education," Georgia State put the place for the experience in mutual territory. Could such a project be as successful at either of the other three territories? Following the findings of Alfie Kohn and other cooperation educators, such could come to pass. The economic factor, which has not been addressed, is focused here. However, being clear on goals which focus more on serving people than solving problems, this too is possible.

Something was begun in this experiment which makes for a good that is democratic. Knowledge is becoming available pertaining to a significant part of the population. These people, the elderly, as generous as they may be, must not be denied opportunity to contribute their resources. Also, they should not be neglected or denied the attention and services needed as a result of declines in physical and mental competence. The future will tell us what was learned from researching this territory—the elderly.

PART 2:
GERONTOLOGICAL
AND THEOLOGICAL
DISCIPLINES AND PRACTICES

The curriculum for the spring term in the GITE project consisted of a series of presentations and panel discussions. The topics dealt with theological disciplines and clergy practices as they related to the concerns of older persons. The presenters were chosen primarily from the three Atlanta seminaries. In addition, faculty members from the same field became panel members to participate in discussions of the issues. The post-doctoral fellows presided and guided the lively interchanges.

In almost all cases, the participants commented on the fact that little was available in their disciplines or practices related to older persons. This high level program excited the faculty and students.

The themes ranged from systematic theology (Ted Runyon) to preaching (Fred Craddock). They covered church history (Gonzalez), New Testament (Pherigo), pastoral care (Gerkin), congregational programs (Trimmer and Styles), worship (Costen), spirituality (Johnson), and churches and communities (Thomas).

This is a large sweep of theological curriculum focussed on the needs and concerns of older persons and how clergy could be involved in ministries to, with and by them.

45

Aging and a Meaningful Future

Theodore H. Runyon, DTheol

SUMMARY. An analysis of some theological resources older persons may use in seeking a meaningful future. Pilgrimage, covenant, baptism and hope are woven into a tapestry of meaning for the elderly.

One of the basic problems that accompanies retirement is the problem of meaning: the way life fits together, makes sense, and has value, purpose and a future. Most of us find our personal identity and much of the meaning of our lives in our jobs (even if we claim we don't like them) and our families (even if they are the source of tensions and frustrations). When the family is grown up and gone, and the familiar routine of the job and workplace is over, the meaning and purpose of life also is threatened.

Not surprisingly, the result is often "retirement depression," for human beings are creatures of meaning and require a meaningful context in order to stay healthy. One of the major differences between human beings and other animals is that lower animals are pre-programmed by their instincts. Their pattern of behavior is set for them by factors over which they have little or no control. Instinct substitutes for meaning. Not so with human beings, who are described by anthropologists as "instinct poor."[1] As important as instincts may be for habitual conduct,[2] our conscious life is largely controlled by that amazing computer with which we have been endowed, located at the top end of our spine. Our brains make it possible for us to react and respond in creative and innovative ways to a variety of circumstances with which we are confronted, and

Theodore H. Runyon is Professor of Systematic Theology at Candler School of Theology, Emory University.

even to override instinct when necessary. As a result, human beings have been able to adapt and adjust more successfully to a variety of conditions, circumstances and climates than any other creature.

The price we pay for this adaptability is that, in comparison with other animals, instinct plays a less powerful role in organizing and directing our lives. Instead, we rely on our extra cranial capacity to order and reorder daily existence and longer term goals in a way not possible for other animals. Many animals remember the past; but humans can also anticipate the future. The negative side of this is, however, that we need a meaningful future. We need goals and purposes in terms of which further life makes sense. When this purposeful context is no longer present our humanity is threatened; what we do no longer fits into a larger pattern that gives direction to our lives.

At the thirty-fifth reunion of my college class this past summer, I was startled to discover that many of my classmates had either recently retired or were planning early retirement prior to age 60! Some had made their pile and were now retiring to "enjoy it." Others were retiring early because consolidations and mergers in their businesses meant that there was no longer a place for them. Supplied by their companies with a "golden parachute," they would land softly someplace in Florida, move into a condo ("no more grass to mow, weeds to pull, or flowers to tend") and look forward to a future of twenty, thirty or forty years in which to play golf, play cards, and watch TV. Affluence has made a retirement lifestyle possible which seems enviable—but is it? I was reminded of an article in which an animal psychologist reported that most American dogs suffer from acute boredom.[3] Traditionally, dogs have had jobs to do. They have herded sheep, guarded livestock, or foraged for food for themselves and their young. But modern dogs in the urban environment are mostly kept in the house where they are pampered and fed—and are dreadfully bored. No wonder, said the psychologist, that they bark and chew the furniture and are suffering from increased illness, both physical and psychological. A steady diet of golf, card-playing and watching TV for twenty or thirty years will predictably have some of the same results. We already know that retirement brings for many persons more rapid deterioration of health than would be the case if they had activities which both they and society deem to be significant. While, like a dog scratching fleas, they can stay busy with things to do, if society views their activities as low priority busywork, many retirees will suffer from the same symptoms as the canine population.

THE LOSS OF RELIGIOUS MEANING

What has gone largely unnoticed is the effect of modern secularization on the meaning quotient of older people today. Religion has traditionally provided a sense of a meaningful future, a context of eternity, so that what one does in this life counts for more than this life, and the future remains a source of hope and promise right up to the end. In earlier generations, the "language of Zion" was a common cultural heritage present in the consciousness of everyone. Remnants of that past can be seen in the verses of familiar hymns. Some hymns are devoted entirely to the transition from this world to the next.

> Lead kindly light amid the circling gloom
> Lead thou me on!
> The night is dark and I am far from home;
> Lead thou me on!
> 'Til the night is gone;
> And with the morn, those angel faces smile,
> Which I have loved long since and lost a while.

Other hymns use the final verse to direct us heavenward. Typical is "Guide me, O Thou great Jehovah":

> When I tread the verge Jordan
> Bid my anxious fears subside
> Death of death and hell's destruction
> Land me safe on Canaan's side
> Songs of praises, songs of praises,
> I will ever give to thee
> I will ever give to thee.

Or the final verse of "Jesus, Savior, pilot me":

>   When at last I near the shore
>   And the fearful breakers roar,
>   Twixt me and the peaceful rest
>   Then while leaning on thy breast
>   May I hear Thee say to me,
>   "Fear not, I will pilot thee."

Even a rousing hymn like "Stand up, stand up for Jesus" has as its final verse:

>   The strife will not be long,
>   This day the noise of battle,
>   The next, the victor's song.
>   To him that overcometh,
>   A crown of life shall be,
>   He with the King of Glory
>   Shall reign eternally.

These songs have shaped the consciousness of a large portion of the American population and are a part of us, whether we realize it or not. They are the substance upon which we fed, beginning in earliest years of Sunday School. And yet the heaven of which they speak is less a matter of intense consciousness for today's older generation than it was for generations past. The dominant cultural determiners, the media and the schools (the sources which feed constant input into the computers of our minds and build up the memory bank of the future), have been largely sanitized of explicit references to religion in order to avoid controversy in our religiously plural society. As a result, we no longer have a common language for the larger context within which this life is lived and the destiny toward which it is directed. The sense of the reality of heaven, its possibility and nearness — and also the shadow side, the recognition of judgement and the possibility of hell — are not what they once were. Many would say, "Good riddance! A morbid preoccupation with heaven and hell was detrimental to humanity." That may be; what is not so apparent is the price paid for the resulting loss of the sense of the eternal. Consciousness of eternity provided a transcendent goal for this life that could not be dimmed by retirement but rather burned more brightly after alternative sources of illumination—job and family—had been extinguished.

Theology itself may be partially to blame for this weakening sense of the reality of heaven. New Testament scholars and theologians have argued persuasively that in the New Testament the "kingdom of God" (referred to by St. Matthew's Gospel as the "kingdom of heaven") is not so much another world after this life as it is the mighty reign of God that comes from heaven to earth to invade and transform conditions in this world. This is of course what we have always prayed ("Thy kingdom come, thy will be done on earth as it is in heaven"), but it did not occur to us that heaven really had to do with the remaking of this world's political and economic orders. Now the discovery that the kingdom of heaven applies to this world rather than exclusively to the next seems to shift heaven's relevance from the older generation to the younger, to those who can still do something about this world.

Moreover, biblical scholars have also introduced uncertainties about traditional notions of life after death. Oscar Cullmann points out that the biblical notion of life after death is not immortality of the soul, as is popularly assumed by most Christian congregations.[4] If there is life after death it is the gift of God and comes with the general resurrection of the dead. This was the dominant Jewish understanding at the time of the writing of the New Testament—not the later, popular hellenistic Greek notion of an innate, immortal soul that by its nature cannot die. The biblical view, argues Cullmann, is that when we die, we die completely. The soul as well as the body loses the life principle, the breath of God.

These biblical and theological findings have tended to add to the pressures of secularization to undermine folk religion and introduce confusion regarding the framework of meaning between retirement and death. Justifiable criticisms aside, "Get right with God!" had the virtue of setting an agenda in anticipation of judgement. If there were debts to pay, they ought to be settled. If estrangements had arisen, they should be overcome. If a kind word needed to be said or a deed done, it could not wait—for the end could come at any time. The hymns and prayers were a constant reminder of that fact. Now the awareness of the end is repressed, the reality of death is denied, and the thought of judgment indefinitely postponed. The cost of this reality-denying conspiracy is the loss of meaning and intensity. If there is no consciousness of the end, the phenomenon of timelessness takes over: every day is like every other day. The sense of time as setting limits within which things must be accomplished is lost, and with it the initiative to make the day count. Without any positive anticipation of the future, the "waiting-to-die" syndrome sets in. What is lost is not just the future but a meaningful present.

RECOVERY OF RELIGIOUS MEANING

If there is an exception to this general decline in the ability of religion in America to provide a direction and purpose for human existence, it is to be found in the Black church where there is no dichotomy between "marching to Zion" and marching from Selma to Montgomery, or from Atlanta to Forsyth County. "We're marching upward to Zion, Zion, the beautiful city of God," contains an implicit political agenda: the overcoming of this world, the transformation of the present order in the light of God's justice, using the present moment to make a difference in the future. Moreover, those marching and those cheering them on were not doing it simply as individuals. They were part of a larger movement; their lives were integrated into a historical destiny that gave significance to their contribution and insured that what they did would live beyond their own numbered years.

Obviously, life after retirement cannot be lived with the intensity of the civil rights movement—nor should it be. Retirees have the right to slow down and enjoy life at a less frantic pace. The question rather is whether there are clues and a pattern in the Black church that could be helpful for determining how religion could be a source of valid and renewed meaning to the aging. Is there a theological contribution to be made which the secularization process is in danger of obscuring? If so, what are the factors that, from a theological standpoint, must be taken into consideration in identifying dependable sources of meaning.

First, meaning that serves as a continuing source of inspiration is seldom privatistic. Meaning requires a supportive community and a common celebration of values. It cannot be maintained indefinitely in isolation, as sociologists of knowledge have pointed out.[5] This is why the amassing of private wealth and security can never guarantee the life of meaning which retirees assume it will. The possessor requires at the very least others who admire and envy his or her self-sufficiency—which of course means that he or she is not self-sufficient at all but dependent upon the envy of others, an unenviable position to be in! The fact that in the long run society does not applaud a life lived only for self is what makes the "ideal" retirement regimen—golf, cards, TV—finally unsatisfying. The internalized values of the larger society are a silent but persistent witness against it. One can defend oneself by joining a subculture of the like-minded; this is the traditional solution of the luxury retirement community or yacht club. However, a progressively narrowing world of relationships and interests is a characteristic problem connected with aging. If one voluntarily narrows significant contacts to fellow members of a single subculture, one has in effect advanced the aging process. The source of one's meaning must open up the world rather than narrow it down in order successfully to combat meaninglessness.

Second, applied to religion this implies that the kind of religious language and symbols that are most meaningful are those not narrowly religious. They are those which apply to life in the world to illumine and transform it, rather than ideas and practices restricted to the internal life of the religious institution itself. The Black church illustrates the case in point. The language of Zion is authentic insofar as it links concrete issues of life in the world with the ultimate context, the widest horizon, within which they occur. As "we're marching to Zion," speaks of the heavenly Jerusalem, it opens up this life to the widest horizons of which it is capable. As it describes another world it is always speaking at the same time of this world and its transformation according to a transcendent and universal standard of justice. Its intention is thus neither privatistic nor narrowly churchly. Black religion loses itself in the service of a larger cause—and thus finds its own authentic mode of being.

However, a third criterion for religiously grounded meaning must be added. To function effectively meaning must be deeply personal without being privatistic. Again, the Black church is an illustration.

A faith that is conscious of standing both in eternity and at a crucial point in history is a faith that links persons both to time and to eternity. It is an "ultimate concern" (Paul Tillich). That with which faith is concerned is experienced as absolute and ultimate; and at the same time the ultimate is perceived as having a stake in the finite situation. Such a faith is both deeply personal and not limited by the personal. It knows it has to do with the objective reality of God's justice in this world and beyond.

Fourth, because change threatens the world of older persons, a source of meaning must be able to put change in a positive context. While fully cognizant of the problems which it creates, change can be welcomed for the promise that it brings rather than feared as undermining present stability.

Are there sources of meaning within the predominant religious tradition in our society, Christianity, which can meet these criteria and thereby serve the needs of older people who require solidly grounded meaning to sustain them in a world that for them is gradually disintegrating? Are there themes and images in the tradition that are understandable and believable, which could infuse and inform life, and put it in a context of continuing significance?

PILGRIMAGE AND COVENANT

Two interrelated pictures which generations of Christians have found compelling are pilgrimage and covenant. One of the earliest names for Christianity was "the Way" (Acts 9:2; 19:9,23; 24:22). And Christian existence was understood as the life of a people "on the way." That gave them a sense that life has a direction and goal; every moment along the way does not stand by itself but is related to that future. And it reminded them that they had not yet arrived; there was always more that lay ahead.

This notion of pilgrimage is of course subject to misunderstanding, and has in fact been misunderstood in many churches whenever it has been reduced to: "I'm just a pilgrim passing through this weary land. Heaven's my home." To be sure, the kingdom of God is the goal, but not in such a way as to deprive this world of significance. Feuerbach's critique of religion has to be taken seriously. His contention was that religion, in order to make God great, robs life in this world of significance, and that the importance of heaven necessarily drains this world of meaning.[6] But this need not be the case. Black religion, often accused of being escapist, demonstrates the opposite. In the Black church at its best, the other world lends this world meaning as struggles taking place here are put in their eternal context and are thus raised to a higher level. The kingdom of God provides not only the goal but also the criterion of every step along the way of our human pilgrimage. It is not a matter of robbing this world of its intrinsic meaning, but rather seeing this world as the object of God's creation, preservation, and new order of justice and truth in which God's will is done both in heaven and on earth.

The theme of pilgrimage is deep-rooted in the Hebrew scriptures. The two chief figures in the Old Testament and progenitors of the nation of Israel, Abraham and Moses, were pilgrims whose faith, as well as the faith of the people they led, was shaped by the faithfulness of the God who promised to be with them on the way. They left the security they had known and ventured forth into the unknown on the basis of Yahweh's promises and presence, symbolized in the Exodus by the ark of the covenant that accompanied them, and by the pillar of cloud that led them by day and the pillar of fire by night.

The gods of the tribes which surrounded the Hebrews were agricultural gods whose power was associated with fixed shrines and holy places. When these tribes were forced out of familiar surroundings, the dislocation was traumatic because in effect they lost their local gods. The Hebrews, by contrast, were sustained on their pilgrimage by the covenant relation to Yahweh. That covenant was a contract of mutual faithfulness, an agreement entered into by Yahweh, who had graciously chosen the nation of Israel to be "a people of his own possession, out of all the peoples that are on the face of the earth" (Deut. 7:6), and pledged faithfulness to them. For its part, Israel was pledged to be loyal to Yahweh, to keep his commandments, and thus to demonstrate to the world what a nation obedient to God and the law of the covenant could become, not only in themselves but as a blessing to other nations. Although the classic form of covenant was the one made with Moses, forged in the Exodus, tested in the wilderness and codified in the commandments, the covenant model for the relationship with God was read back by the Hebrews into the progenitors of the nation, Abraham, Noah and even Adam. This pledge of Yahweh to his people, and the pledge of the people to their God, provided identity and security. The covenant principle meant certainty in the midst of flux and continuity in the midst of change. According to the tradition, when Abraham set out from Haran "by faith . . . , not knowing where he was to go" (Heb. 11:8), he was seventy-five years old (Gen. 12:4); and Moses at the time when he led the Hebrews out of Egypt was about eighty (Deut. 31:2). They were not youngsters, even by Old Testament standards. Yet they ventured into the unknown with confidence, relying on the faithfulness of the covenant God who called them into pilgrimage.

Yahweh did not promise them a short journey, or easy victories, or protection from adversity, but he did promise his presence with them through it all. Indeed, one interpretation of the proper translation of the self-disclosure of the sacred name of Yahweh is not the cryptic, "I am that I am," but "I will be with you" (Ex. 3:13).[7] Yet this covenant relationship was not privatistic. Each Jew did not go on a pilgrimage alone; they were bound to Yahweh with a covenant that called the nation to obedience. And each individual had a calling within the call of the whole people. Yet it was an intensely personal calling; each person and family unit was responsible directly to Yahweh for fulfilling their part of the covenant obligation. "Choose this day whom you will serve" (Josh. 24:15).

The guidelines for the relationship were to be found in the law of the covenant which set down conditions that could not be fulfilled simply by religious observances and rites but required justice, mercy and truth in everyday dealings with one's neighbors. The rights of the poor, the weak and the powerless in the society were to be respected. And one's relationship to God could not be separated from these ordinary this-worldly duties.

This biblical understanding of life as an ongoing pilgrimage, lived within the supporting structure of a covenant relationship with the Source of all life in this world and the next, holds much promise as a source of meaning which is communal and not privatistic, which applies to life in this world as well as lending this world eternal significance by incorporating it into the relationship with the divine. And it assures the divine presence on the way, providing continuity in the midst of change.

BAPTISM

The notion of covenant continues as a strong motif in the New Testament. In the Christian context the sign of the covenant is baptism, which marks both the beginning and the continuing basis for the Christian journey. Those who are baptized are invited into the covenant relation by God, made part of "a holy nation, God's own people," the new "Israel of God," those who have received the mercy and love of God and have thereby been made "new creatures" and the first signs of a new creation (I Pet. 2:9; Gal. 6:16). Baptism is a rite that is virtually universal among Christians and is practiced by all churches that observe sacraments or ordinances. Moreover, for practicing Christians it is an event in their own lives of which they are continually reminded as they participate in the baptism of others and are called to "Remember your baptism!" Whenever they witness baptism, the meaning of it is made present and visible. It is not just an abstract concept. It is a meaning-event in the life of the person, the family, and the community.

Like the covenant it symbolizes, baptism meets the criteria for a fundamental source of significance. It is highly personal. Each of the billions of Christians baptized over the past two millennia has been the focus of an act in which the covenantal faithfulness of God was promised, and a foundation for the life of that person was laid in the grace and presence of God. At the same time, it is not privatistic but communal, for the act incorporates the person into a fellowship described in the New Testament as the "Body of Christ," the community created to carry on Christ's own ministry of prophetic questioning, healing, reconciling and redeeming, in the world today. It is therefore not a rite whose meaning is restricted to religious observance alone but extends into every aspect of the world's life and lends transcendent significance to even the most menial acts: "Inasmuch as ye did it unto one of the least of these my brethren, ye did it unto me" (Matt. 25:40). Finally, baptism is a spiritual undergirding for life that sustains and supports from beginning to end. Regardless of when in life it occurs, baptism is the reminder of human dependence upon the Creator without which life would be impossible. It is also the sign of God's faithfulness to the covenant and promise to accompany us through all the vicissitudes of this life and beyond, providing continuity to our journey and a future which cannot be snatched from us — not even by death itself.

HOPE AND THE FUTURE

We turn now to focus on the future, to that which is yet to be, because this is the dimension that proves so problematic for many older persons. Up to this point in their lives, the hope that is the necessary energy of life has been generated by anticipating the future, imagining goals, plans and achievements that with time can be reached. Retirement itself is often such an objective. But what happens when the future becomes uncertain and goals and plans seem hollow and unrealistic, an exercise in futility? As the Catholic philosopher and paleontologist, Teilhard de Chardin, has pointed out, there is no "energy of despair. . . . All conscious energy is . . . founded on hope."[8] Yet despair, the lack of hope and meaning, is what stalks the lives of many of the elderly as the difficulties of continued life increase while the meaning of it decreases.

Paul Pruyser, a psychiatrist with the Menninger Foundation, in an article entitled "Maintaining Hope in Adversity,"[9] points out how hope is a valuable asset precisely in the most hopeless of circumstances, in terminal illness. He speaks of a hypothetical case where the person has been told by the physician, or has surmised on the basis of clues, that he has a terminal disease, and that there is nothing more that medical science can do. There is no cure available and a downhill course seems inevitable. The patient could react in one of two ways to that kind of news, says Pruyser.

Let's assume that this patient is a realistic person who has insight into the seriousness of his condition, has never been prone to fooling himself, and is a planner who likes to anticipate things and cover himself against the worst. As a possible reaction, this patient may squarely face his fate, and ostensibly give up all hope. He phases out his earlier plans and ambitions, preparing himself for the demise that is surely and soon to come. Most physicians and other helping professionals would quickly point out that such a reaction, though not unrealistic, would be very likely to hasten the downhill course of the disease and make the patient particularly difficult to treat.

A second possible reaction would be for the patient to accept the diagnosis and the prognosis, to see their inescapable implications, to realize that nature has its laws and is more powerful than the individual, but yet, to hope! Health professionals would point out that such a set of attitudes is likely to retard, if not stem, the course of the illness, for they would know that under their influence, the patient is mobilizing all the organism's resources and defenses, thereby enhancing and possibly prolonging his life. Moreover, this patient would be seen as more gratifying to treat, to care for or to attend to. His readiness to receive help enhances the helpers' eagerness to help, and may even make them more inventive in their helping maneuvers.[10]

But how can such a hope be engendered when the actual fate of everything, from the smallest cell to the planet itself, is death? Are not those most realistic who simply come to terms with the final hopelessness of life—and while away the hours playing golf, or cards, or watching TV? Not if the God of the Exodus pilgrimage and the covenant, the God of Jesus and the kingdom, is God—i.e., is the ultimate context within which our lives are set. If this God is God, then every moment of our lives, including life in anticipation of death, is a living out of our baptism. It is lived in the presence of God, in vocation, in calling, in service. And every moment is lived toward the future, which is always filled with meaning, even in the midst of suffering and death, because it is always filled with the presence of the god whose kingdom is coming to meet us. As William F. Lynch points out, hope is relational.[11] It is not something we can produce out of ourselves. Therefore, it is worse than useless to tell people to pull themselves up by their own bootstraps and to hope. Hope is not an interior resource, which needs nothing but itself. Hope depends upon a relationship with a Source beyond ourselves that can give us an ultimate future, a future upon which we can rely up to the moment of death and beyond. This hope is a necessity for the quality of life—life that can constantly receive hope from the God who calls us into being with baptism, guides us on the way, and receives us at the end of the journey into the kingdom that incorporates and preserves our lives and transcends death. Hope is not the product of the quantity of time we have left, therefore, but of the quality of the relationships, divine and human, in which we spend it.

Hope and meaning are thus seen to be closely related and mutually interdependent. Moreover, the connection between the two enables us to respond to an objection that could be legitimately raised against this whole discussion of the importance of meaning in the aging process. Does not the focus on meaning reflect a middle-class bias in favor of the rational and ideational? Is not the search for meaning much more characteristic of the college-educated and affluent? Does it apply to the aging across the board?

The discussion of hope should demonstrate that meaning is much more than its rational component. It is not simply the product of the reflective mind operating in terms of its own resources and making sense out of things. Much more it is a rich texture of relationships in which we receive affirmation and value from outside ourselves, from sources both human and divine. It is these relationships that are captured in biblical pictures of "pilgrimage" and "covenant" and the sign-event of baptism, and that give rise to a community which not only shares ideas but feeds the hungry, houses the stranger, and visits the sick, the imprisoned (Matt. 25:35f) and, dare we add, the elderly?!

The meaning which Christianity has to offer to the aging is therefore the same as it offers to all persons, namely, a community of meaning and mutual service which is grounded in the transcendent and mediates by word and deed a fundamental understanding.

These are some of the theological resources which can prove useful in the discussion with gerontology of the threat posed by the loss of meaning and purpose in the lives of retirees. To be meaningful, life must be seen in a larger context. And healthy religion provides that context along with a community to sustain the aging on their journey. This is important not just for the elderly among us but for everyone, regardless of our calendar age. For we are all "on the way."

NOTES

1. Arnold Gehlen, *Anthropologische Forschung* (Hamburg: Rowohlt), 1961, p. 17f.

2. Cf. Konrad Lorenz, *On Aggression* (New York: Harcourt, Brace and World), 1966, p. 236ff.

3. Chet Fuller, "Urban Dog's Life No Cat's Meow," *Atlanta Constitution* (Sept. 22, 1986), p. 10-A.

4. Oscar Cullmann, *Immortality of the Soul or Resurrection of the Dead?* (New York: Macmillan), 1958.

5. Peter L. Berger & Thomas Luckmann, *The Social Construction of Reality* (Garden City, NY: Doubleday), 1967.

6. Ludwig Feuerbach, *The Essence of Christianity* (New York: Harper), 1957.

7. Martin Buber, *Konigtum Gottes* (Heidelberg: Lambert Schneider), 1956, p. 69.

8. Pierre Teilhard de Chardin, *The Phenomenon of Man* (London: Collins Fontana), 1959, p. 256.

9. Paul Pruyser, "Maintaining Hope in Adversity," *Pastoral Psychology*, Vol. 35, No. 2 (Winter 1986), pp. 120-131.

10. *Ibid.*, p. 124f.

11. William F. Lynch, *Images of Hope* (Baltimore: Helicon), 1965, p. 159ff.

An Historical Perspective on the Church and the Elderly

Catherine Gunsalus Gonzalez, PhD

SUMMARY. Historically, the roles of church and society have changed with respect to the treatment of the elderly. These changes are traced. Beginning with the New Testament times, the shifts are reviewed in the Roman period, the Germanic invasions, the High Middle Ages, and the urbanized industrial times which reach into the present.

There are very few resources on the topic of the attitude toward the elderly and the treatment of them in the history of the church. If one does not look for the exact topic, but rather seeks tangents that touch it, the search is more fruitful. What I propose to do, therefore, is to explore a variety of entrances into the given subject, rather than pursue a more logically developed presentation. First, we will look at a helpful issue from the history of doctrine, and then at elements of the institutional history of the church. Lastly, we will look at cultural changes that have altered the situation of the elderly both within and outside of the church.

THEOLOGICAL ISSUES

Augustine is clearly one of the most significant theologians for the development of the western theological tradition, Catholic and Protestant alike. As elucidated by Karl Rahner in *The Theology of Death*, there are aspects of Augustine's theological anthropology that can be very useful indeed for the question of the elderly.

Catherine Gunsalus Gonzalez is Professor of Church History, Columbia Theological Seminary.

Augustine deals quite creatively with the basic question: Did God so create human beings that they would age? Is aging—and old age in particular—the intention of God, a part of the good creation? And if it is, how then do we understand the unpleasant, painful, and heart-rending characteristics that often accompany old age in our own experience?

Augustine contends that God created human beings who would age, and who would eventually, like ripe fruit ready to fall from the tree, be ready to leave this world in which God had placed them, ready for the next stage of life that is to be lived in glory with God. It would be a process of "consummation" rather than death. This process has been corrupted by sin, as has every other characteristic of human life, but we can have a glimmer of what that consummation would be in the occasional "good death" that still shows the original intention of the creator.

Such a death would be at an appropriate age, when one's life has been lived with significance and contribution to the wider society. It would be a death that looked to the world beyond this life without fear and with a joyful anticipation. It would be a death that was faced knowingly and with time to make farewells to family and friends, to bring one's life to a fitting and loving conclusion.

Such a death is no longer the universal expectation of humanity, even for those who are faithful. Death comes at an early age, for children, for those who are in the prime of their years of contribution, or even just beginning. Nor is death always a painless consummation and free of fear. Death does not give notice, but may come unexpectedly, without time for farewells. These are not characteristics that God had intended, but rather the corruption of human life due to the fall of creation. These are the result of sin—not simply the sin of that particular individual, but the fallenness of the whole creation, which, like the rain, affects the just and unjust alike. Yet by faith, which includes the forgiveness of sin, there can, on occasion, be glimpses of what had been intended.

There is an excellent example of such a "good death" in the description of the death of the nineteenth century theologian, Friedrich Schleiermacher, in the study done by Martin Redeker. Schleiermacher became ill with pneumonia, while a famous and still active theologian. He had said earlier in his life that he wished to be alert and conscious when death overtook him, able to meet it without surprise. That happened. He gathered his household around his bedside, except for the young children. He celebrated communion. After he had said the words of institution, he said: "To these words of Scripture I hold fast. They are the foundation of my faith." He finished the communion prayer, and said: "In this love and communion we will remain one." Then he died, and around his bed, with the children now present, everyone received communion.[1]

According to Augustine, such a death retains certain characteristics of the consummation anticipated in the original creation. There is no fear; the transition to a new life has the willed support of the person; it includes the verbal leave-taking and witness that really sums up the person's life.

Yet we are not in Eden. Something drastic has happened. Death is an enemy, an unwelcome guest, it does not come at the right time, and fear is a fairly constant accompaniment. Disease and suffering have resulted. Guilt and fear have resulted. Except by faith, we do not know what lies beyond this life. Except by faith, we cannot be certain that the sinful life which is reaching its consummation, will be forgiven the sin and given the grace to receive a future undeserved. Schleiermacher's death shows that faith. His death shows a glimpse of the originally intended consummation but under the conditions of a fallen world.

To Augustine, aging is natural and to be expected. It is part of God's good creation. The process of aging should lead to a natural consummation. Under the conditions of a fallen creation, many people will not go far in the aging process—they will die young. But some will go far along on that road. Many will not age well, but will suffer debilitating disease. Yet in all of this, by faith, there can be glimpses of that intended process, even under these warped conditions. The church offers the faith that lets this be seen.

There is something very important here about the mission of the church to the aging. Even when death is not expected immediately, it says something about the leave-taking that is necessary, the loving relationships that need to be nurtured or re-established where there has been estrangement. If the vision of what was intended can be seen clearly, then whatever can be done in the midst of the given situation—which may be much or little—can be imagined and pursued. Without that vision, little can be done.

Our culture sees an instantaneous death as more of a "blessing" than a death that comes with plenty of warning. Our medical practice makes it difficult for a dying person to be surrounded by family and friends, to be conscious and die with some sense of participating willingly in the process. We do not see that as a "good death."

Until about the fifteenth century, meditation on death was built into the liturgy of the church, not for the elderly more than for any other group. However, beginning in the fifteenth century, there was an assumption that after about age forty, one ought to begin the preparation for death, and be consciously prepared to make the final choice—at the moment of death—for God rather than for evil. Books were written on "The Art of Dying."

The situation began to change in the sixteenth century. In Protestant circles, the moment of death was not considered the essential determinant, when faith had been part the of person's life before that. The "good death" of the elderly, in full mental capacity, taking leave of the gathered family, still was the ideal for many. In Roman Catholic circles, the desire to have a priest present so the last rites could be received remained very important, and, therefore, some warning of the approach of death was preferred.

As secularism made its inroads in the succeeding centuries, however, the need for time to prepare for death receded culturally. An instantaneous death, without warning and therefore without suffering, was increasingly seen as good, and this pattern continues for us today.

All of this is theologically significant, and needs to be seen as related to the church's understanding of what it means to be human. If aging is a good thing, even though death stands at the end, the church needs to provide some greater guidance as to how this whole process is to be understood by the faithful community. The definition of a "good death" as understood theologically and as understood culturally needs to be explored and discussed.

INSTITUTIONAL RESPONSES

As an organization, the church has responded in a variety of ways to the needs of the elderly. The earliest witnesses we have are the New Testament references to "the widows" in the early church (Acts 6; I Timothy 5). The Jerusalem Temple supported financially widows from the Diaspora who wished to die in the holy city. The synagogue also supported needy widows in their own community. When such widows became part of the church, the church continued such support.

Furthermore, when women who were part of the church became widowed, they might well have been dependent on non-Christian children, or might have needed to remarry outside of the church. If the congregation supported them, their involvement in the life of the church could continue unimpeded. Once the church had been in a community for several generations, then the situation for widows would have been easier. In fact, we find that by the early second century, the order of widows has been expanded to include younger women who had never married — "the virgins" — who were also supported by the church. By the end of the second century, the virgins were a much larger group to which some widows were added. In the case of both the virgins and the widows, this order included only those women who specifically were enrolled, set apart by a vow and prayer.

These widows were probably older women, and were supported either by money or by the distribution of food and clothing. In return for their support, they played an important role in the life of the congregation, visiting the sick, caring for children, teaching children and other women who wished to become part of the church. They were part of the ministry of the church. When in the second century the virgins began to take over some of these jobs, there was clear unhappiness on the part of the widows that some of their work was being taken from them. In this early period — the second through the fifth centuries — the church discouraged second marriages, so even widows who were young might well have been supported by the church for the rest of their lives.

The church developed many charitable institutions, especially after it became the dominant and official religion of the Roman Empire in the fourth century. The elderly—both men and women—were one of the many groups that might need care in hospitals that cared for the poor in general. These hospitals were under the control of the bishop. Deacons and deaconesses were related to this work. (Simone de Beauvoir points out that there may not have been too many who were both poor and elderly, since in many cultures, the poor die young. Those who survive into old age are more likely not to be poor.)

With the destruction of an urban culture in the West in the early Middle Ages, such formal institutions also died out. This destruction brought new needs and new institutional means to respond to them.

GERMANIC AND ROMAN VIEWS OF THE ELDERLY

The early church, especially in the West, was largely within the borders of the Roman Empire. Beginning in the fourth century, however, that Empire began to crumble, invaded by wave after wave of Germanic groups—"the Barbarian invasions." The new medieval culture that developed included both Roman and Germanic elements, put into a new form with the active involvement of the church.

The Roman and the Germanic cultures were quite different. Roman law gave legal guarantees as to the ownership of property and the role of the *paterfamilias*—the father of the whole household that included married sons and their families as well as servants, etc. Age did not take away from this authority, for it was upheld by law, and Roman law was the pride of the whole culture. The Germanic tribes were not organized in that fashion. They had for generations developed as warrior groups around a chief. What gave the chief legitimacy was a combination of family ties and physical strength, particularly strength in battle. An elderly chief was therefore always in danger of being supplanted by younger, more vigorous members of the family. A son could show himself more powerful and defeat his father in combat, and therefore take over the leadership role the father had had.

What happened when a church that was largely formed within a

Roman view of the world became a dominant institution in the Germanic world? There were a variety of patterns. But one of the most interesting is the role that monasticism began to play as the haven for the elderly who could retire to monasteries without being defeated by the next generation, and leave the scene of combat gracefully and safely.

In Ireland, this came to be a very clear pattern, and not only for the chiefs. Many Irish homesteads had what was called "the west bedroom" for the parents when the son took over as head of the household, and the position of the parents was not always pleasant. The parents may not have willingly relinquished their role. Irish monasticism often was to be found at the heart of a community. It provided a retirement home for the elderly, as well as a home for those who did not marry. Its chapel was the church for the whole community, and, therefore, the services in the church were family reunions. The elderly retained moral and spiritual authority even while losing—or giving up—authority in the economic and political life of the community.

In the rest of Western Europe, it also was common for those in high positions to retire to the monastic life, though monastic foundations were rural rather than in the center of the society as in Ireland. In both Ireland and the rest of Europe, husbands and wives would have to agree to this, and separate, both taking up the religious vocation. But the alternatives in a culture still dominated by power given to the physically strong, were not all that attractive. In this situation, the church provided a safe haven, a sanctuary for the elderly, within its own monastic structures. This was clearly a new use for monasticism.

In the High Middle Ages, when commerce and wealth increased, monasticism again played an interesting role for the elderly. In the thirteenth century, the Franciscan order developed, with its stress on holy poverty. Wealth was viewed as a possible impediment to salvation, or at least to a "good death." Therefore, as part of the process of preparation for death, many who had been very much a part of the world of commerce during most of their lives, became members of the Third Order, Franciscans. They continued to live in families and as part of the world, but upholding as far as their station in life permitted, the ideals of holy poverty. As these people approached old age, especially if they were widowed, they might well decide to join the first or second order — the full, celibate monastic order for men or women — and die as monastics. This seemed far safer than remaining in the secular world.

This period also saw stress on ministry to the urban poor, that new phenomenon of the return of commerce and urbanization. Since the earlier monastic forms had been largely in the rural areas, they did not meet these new needs. It was for this reason that the new groups, such as the Franciscans, had developed. There was a call for the church to provide institutions for particular groups of the poor, including orphans and the elderly.

In this later period, where wealth rather than physical strength determined one's power in the society, the motivation for entering the monastic life was quite different than it had been earlier. But monasticism had also changed to meet the new situation. In both cases, monasticism had a special attraction for the elderly.

Throughout the medieval period, monasticism was the major vehicle for the church's response to the needs of the elderly, as well as being a place of ministry for the elderly. What was the situation, then, when the Protestant Reformation ended monasticism for a major section of the West?

The family was the expected resource for most of the elderly. The church stressed its authority over the younger generation. It is interesting that in New England, in the Puritan churches, the older members were given the preferred seats at the front of the church, with younger people at the back. This continued until the Industrial Revolution began, at which point the seating had more to do with wealth and position than with age.

Especially among the Puritans in New England a pattern developed of fairly late marriages. When older children were ready to marry and leave home, they were given some land by their parents, and help in setting up their own homes. By the time the youngest child reached the age for marriage, the parents were quite elderly, and this child was expected to remain at home and care for the parents. If the child married, the new family was established in this home, with careful provisions made — legally and documented — as to the rights and expectations of the care to be given to the parents. When the parents died, the child inherited this home. The responsibility of parents for assisting their children in establishing their own homes, was all upheld and strengthened by the church.

By the nineteenth century, the situation had changed. The Industrial Revolution created great mobility, so that parents could not expect their children to stay close and inherit the home. Urbanization grew, as did the problem of urban poverty. The same was true in Europe. Within Protestantism, without the formal monastic structures of the Catholic Church, new forms of ministry to the elderly developed, particularly in Germany. These were the orders of deaconesses, which had an almost monastic character to them. Deaconesses had their origin in German Pietist circles. They established homes for the elderly poor, and specific ministries to them. In this country, the movement spread from German Methodists to the rest of Methodism that had its origin in England. It also was to be found in German Reformed groups that had come to this country. The Deaconess movement provided a full-time, set apart ministry for women to a variety of people marginalized by the rapid urban growth. With the more recent opening of all ministries of the church to women, the place of the specific role of deaconesses has become problematic, along with the form of ministry that they had performed.

SOME SOCIOLOGICAL COMMENTS

One can divide the period of western church history into four sections, with the first and third showing similarities, and the second and fourth having some interesting comparisons. I would call the first period the time of the church within the Roman Empire, from the first to the fifth centuries. The elderly retained their economic status regardless of their age. Society was stable in this regard. Money gave status within the family, and as long as the father — or parents — controlled the money, their security in the society remained unchanged.

The second period is that of the Germanic invasions and the upheavals that came with the emerging new European society. Power was not based on money, but on strength and ability to fight or work in the fields. When strength faded, so did position in the family. The elderly could find themselves dispossessed and displaced.

The third period is that of the High Middle Ages, and the return of a clear money economy. Again, power could be retained by the elderly because of the economic base they retained. In many respects, their situation was like that of the Roman Empire. This situation increased in the sixteenth century, and remained typical of the period up through the seventeenth century. When the Industrial Revolution began, and particularly as it became the dominant force in the nineteenth century, there was a recurrence of the situation of the early medieval period, but with a difference. The elderly were readily displaced, not because of physical weakness, but because of the constant explosion of knowledge and skills. Parents could not teach their children the skills they would need in the market place, for the skills were new, and constantly developing. The elderly were a drain on the productive economy, no longer contributing. Unless they were wealthy, and had retained power because of money, they could find themselves in dire straits.

The elderly then became a burden for the family, as did children. In an industrial society, where knowledge is the key to power, and knowledge is something parents cannot teach but only schools can, children are a financial drain rather than a financial asset to a family. The people who are working, particularly in their most productive years, find themselves financially responsible for both the education of their children, which becomes more and more extensive, and the care of their parents. This is the "middle" character of middle age! Many elderly are put very much into the situation of the elderly in the second period of our history, and neither the society nor the church has found good responses to this new situation. Now we are hearing of situations of the abuse of the elderly within families, and many need a safe haven that has not developed. The elderly who fare well are those who can maintain the character of the first and third period: keeping power through maintaining financial security.

CONCLUSION

The church's ministry to the elderly, as well as its attitudes toward the elderly and the role they can play within the life of the church, has not been static. The church has responded to cultural situations it did not create, and needs to continue doing so. In the message it gives to the whole society, in the values it seeks to implant in its own members, there needs to be a clear addressing of the needs of the elderly in our own day. What institutional forms can this take? In some ways, the budding hospice movement has characteristics of the earlier monasticism, and it needs to be seen in this light. But there are other needs that have not been addressed. A look at the way in which the church has faced such challenges in the past can be a beginning point for dealing with the issues that face us today.

NOTE

1. Martin Redeker, *Schleiermacher: Life and Thought*. (Philadelphia: Fortress Press), 1973, p. 212.

Gerontology and the New Testament

Lindsey P. Pherigo, PhD

SUMMARY. The New Testament does not center attention on elders more than others. Yet, some interesting ideas and approaches are reviewed, including intriguing questions for teaching plans for use with older persons in studying the scriptures.

The emergence of gerontology as a special discipline has affected New Testament studies in much the same way that the new consciousness-level about sexist discrimination against women has affected it. One could add racism to the general picture as well. In all these instances, what has happened is that New Testament studies now are more aware of the presence and function of these new factors. The gerontological revolution has given rise to special attention to the older persons in the New Testament writings and to the implications of their story for our own times.

INDIVIDUAL OLDER PERSONS IN THE NEW TESTAMENT

References to the elderly in the New Testament are of several kinds. There is, first of all, a number of specific elderly persons who are simply story subjects. In the beginning of the Gospel of Luke the priest Zachariah and his wife Elizabeth are featured in a story about the conception of John the Baptizer (1:5-25). This story parallels, in some respects, the Old Testament stories of the conception and birth of Isaac to the aged Abraham and Sarah (Genesis 17:1-21; 18:1-15; 21:1-7). It is followed by two other stories featur-

---

Lindsey P. Pherigo is Professor of New Testament and Early Church History, Emeritus, Saint Paul School of Theology.

75

ing elderly persons, Simeon (Luke 2:25-35) and Anna (2:36-38). The exemplary piety of all these persons, excepting only Zachariah's initial skepticism (paralleling Abraham's, or Sarah's, skepticism), is implicitly held up as a model for elderly persons in general, and they are affirmed as important characters in the story, age notwithstanding, but no further gerontological application seems appropriate.

The elderly Moses is mentioned in the speech of Stephen in Acts 7:30-36. There the only point of gerontological concern is also implicit. It reminds the reader that the religious significance of Moses for the Israelites began when he was 80 years old, and that his leadership spanned the period from age 80 to age 120.

Paul used the elderly Abraham as a model of faith (Romans 4:1-22). By contrast, the Epistle of James uses him as a model of works (2:21). In Hebrews (Chapter 11) the famous list of persons who illustrate faith includes the elderly Enoch, Abraham, Sarah, Jacob, and Joseph.

These specific persons, although older persons, do little or nothing for the questing gerontologist. They are simply exemplars of piety, or faith, or of continuing significance into old age.

OLDER PERSONS IN GENERAL

In Judaism "the elders" had distinctive importance. Although they were officials they were also actually old persons. Judaism, unlike later Christianity, never had younger "elders." These Jewish elders are frequently mentioned in the New Testament. They are the bearers of tradition (Mark 7:3, 5 and parallels in Matthew) and also authoritative in some way in current affairs (Matthew 16:21; Acts 5:8 and many other references).

In Christian circles "the elders" continue to function in the same way. They "rule" the church (Acts 11:30, etc.; 1 Timothy 5:17; Titus 1:5; 1 Peter 5:5). Even though "elder" eventually became an office in the church that had only a marginal relation to age, nevertheless in the early stages of the church's organization, its adoption of the synagogue pattern makes it most likely that the earliest Christian "elders" were actually elderly men. The instructions to elders in 1 Peter 5:1-4 not only deals with their leadership role, but does so in contrast to the instructions that follow for younger men.

In one passage, it appears that the elders not only have a ruling function but also are healers (James 5:14).

In the Revelation to John, "twenty-four elders" seem to have a special status in the heavenly court (4:4, 10, etc.), but they are of little gerontological concern. More interesting, even if not applicable to our lives in this age, is the apocalyptic assumption that death is linked with the evil powers of the universe, and will be eliminated in the new age to come. That not only seems to eliminate aging in the new age but makes gerontology itself a specialization subject that belongs only to this age. For present-age gerontological study, regarding death as evil has serious consequences for how we approach it. This position is unfortunate, but there's no solid New Testament data against the death-is-the-enemy viewpoint of the popular apocalyptic theology that is so widespread in the New Testament. Some weak opposition might be culled from Philippians 1:19-26 and Luke 23:43.

The elderly in general deserve the respect due to fathers and mothers (1 Timothy 5:1-2). Jesus is reported as citing approvingly the commandment to honor fathers and mothers (Mark 10:19 and parallels in Matthew and Luke), yet on another occasion he is reported as refusing to let a certain man bury his father (Luke 9:59-60). Disobedience to parents is condemned, along with other evils, in 2 Timothy 3:2. Paul wrote that parents should lay up for their children, not children for their parents (2 Corinthians 12:14), but this is in a defensive context and has a different meaning than it would have as an independent saying. That children should provide for their parents is the lesson of Joseph providing for Jacob (Acts 7:14) and the strong instruction of 1 Timothy 5:8 (which assumes elderly dependents). In much the same vein, the author of the Pastorals gives regulations for the care of "genuine" widows, excluding those less than 60 years old (1 Timothy 5:9) and those who could be cared for by their children or grandchildren (5:4). Whether aged parents or aged widows, the gerontological concern seems limited to a caretaking form of charity. The same mood is reflected in Acts 6:1-3.

Apostolic Age culture assumed a certain wisdom for the elderly.

This wisdom is usually in association with "maturity," which is not necessarily associated with old age. Most of these maturation themes are Pauline (1 Corinthians 2:6; 3; 14:20; Philippians 3:15; Colossians 1:28; Ephesians 4:13-14, etc.) but a strong statement is also in Hebrews (5:11 through 6:3).

SOME MORE GENERAL POINTS

Two statements could be construed as having some bearing on gerontological concerns. "The last shall be first and the first last" (Mark 10:31 and parallels) has an implication that could be developed homiletically, and so also does Paul's statement about the social class typical of the Christians, "God chose what is weak in the world to shame the strong" (1 Corinthians 1:27), but in neither case would good exegesis lead us into gerontological waters.

Another general consideration has more bearing on our present concerns. In several places the New Testament stresses the unity of all Christians. "That they may be one" is an important theme in John 17 (especially verses 20-23). In the Pauline literature the unity of the body of Christ is an important concept (especially 1 Corinthians 12; Romans 12:3-8; Ephesians 4:1-16).

This theme of unity includes the practice of equality among Christians, and the proper exercise of each person's gift in the inclusive community. The gerontological implications are plain: the elderly Christians have gifts to be honored and used, and the elderly are to be fully included in the Body of Christ which is the Church.

While it would probably be unwarranted to attribute to New Testament writers the sociological awarenesses of our time, it is nevertheless apparent that some of them, such as Paul, the author of the Fourth Gospel, and the author of Ephesians (if not Paul) did have at least a rudimentary grasp of the reality of groups as influential on individuals. The maximum exercise of individual gifts is impossible without the support of the community, and gerontologically, that means that the elderly segment needs the full support of the community of Christians. It further means that the community itself cannot come to its maturity without the contributions of the elderly.

"OLD WIVES' TALES"

Perhaps the most pregnant of the New Testament possibilities for gerontological usefulness lies in an element that has been heretofore neglected. It is being uncovered by Dennis MacDonald's research into the apocryphal stories about Paul found outside the New Testament, especially those in the Acts of Paul. He believes that these stories were circulating orally, that they were very popular, and that the author of the Pastoral Epistles knew these stories and deliberately set out to "correct" the "false" impression of Paul that these apocryphal stories cultivated.

In his ground-breaking work, *The Legend and the Apostle*, MacDonald convincingly shows that the Paul of the legends was a social radical, promoting chastity, asceticism (including vegetarianism and abstinence from alcoholic beverages), opposing slavery, encouraging women to leave husbands and lovers, and in general disturbing the established order of society. The Pastorals set about to contradict these stories and to "domesticate" Paul for the Church.

MacDonald further shows that these "legends" about Paul "stand closer to the center of Paul's theology than to the Pastorals" (p. 98). In other words, the legends of a socially radical Paul are probably more accurate historically than the domesticated Paul of the Pastorals.

The gerontological aspect of this disclosure of a socially radical Paul lies in MacDonald's probing into the source of these stories that are "corrected" in the Pastorals. What is this source? How was the tradition of a socially radical Paul kept alive against the concerted efforts of the establishment church? How did the undomesticated Paul of the legends fare against the domesticated Paul of the Pastorals?

The clue is found in the admonition of the Pastorals not to take seriously "old wives' tales" (about Paul?). 1 Timothy 4:7 warns the reader to "avoid the profane tales told by old women." It was indeed the "old women" who kept alive the stories of the socially radical Paul. Instead of perpetuating the troubles Paul caused, the author of the Pastorals instructs old women to "train the young women to love their husbands and . . . to be . . . domestic . . . and submissive to their husbands that the word of God not be discredited" (Titus 2:3-5).

The memory of the actual Paul, preserved and passed on by the "old women" was a valuable contribution, made outside the church's official teachings, and contrary to the church's efforts to show its conformity to the established mores of the Empire. Neither the liberation of slaves nor the liberation of women (the real Paul) served the interests of the second century church, so the most effective way to put out the Pauline brush fires was to use the well-established device of pseudepigraphic writing (the Pastorals). Even though the memory of a socially radical Paul, preserved in the legends, survived for four hundred years in spite of the Pastorals, the ultimate victory of the Pastorals was predestined by their canonical status.

What's the lesson? That "old wives' tales" may preserve much value that would otherwise be sacrificed to the current needs of the organization. There is a striking parallel to this in contemporary medical circles, where the establishment is revising its wholesale condemnation of "folk medicine," also preserved from generation to generation by the "old women."

CONCLUSIONS

Overall, the gerontological aspects of New Testament studies are supplementary rather than central. The Hebrew scriptures are richer here.

In teaching the New Testament, we who teach need to include gerontological concerns among the other peripheral dimensions of New Testament concerns. It certainly would be an unjustified distortion to give such concerns anything like a central position, except, of course, when the study itself is focused on gerontology. It is more important to engage older persons in the study of the New Testament's principal themes than to focus on the aspects which relate more to their age than to their person.

In stressing central New Testament themes, a teaching plan would, of course, include gerontological concerns no matter what the student age-group was. In the case of teaching the New Testament to the elderly, a teaching plan should give full opportunity to two special factors. First, it should assume that the learning abilities of healthy older persons is not restricted. There is little justification for a plan that backs off from controversial issues or avoids things "too difficult" or "upsetting." The elderly have full rights to know the truth and to wrestle with new ideas. Second, a good teaching plan would involve elderly students in the discussion at a higher level than would be appropriate for younger students. This allows the full contribution of the accumulated experience (and sometimes wisdom) of the elderly. This might be especially significant in studies where spiritual maturation is more of a goal than learning new information or dealing with new ideas. The church should provide the environment in which its elderly portion can be fully involved in its ongoing mission, both giving and receiving in an inclusive community. This opens most fully the channels of grace.

To further these special concerns, more research is needed. We need to know more precisely what role the New Testament has played in the lives of older Christians, how much of it they know, and where the unexplored areas are. It would be significant to know why certain parts have risen to special significance while other parts have been overlooked. Is there a pattern here? Is the pattern the same everywhere, or are there regional or denominational patterns? Answers to questions like these would make our teaching of the New Testament to older persons more effective.

Pastoral Care and Models of Aging

Charles V. Gerkin, DD

SUMMARY. Four models of understanding aging persons and of pastoral care of the elderly are proposed: The symmetrical model, a loss/compensation model, an epigenetic model, and a historical/eschatological model. Each is described briefly with implications for pastoral and congregational care of older persons.

If there are two principles that have for centuries informed the pastoral care tradition of both the Christian church and the Jewish community, they are that the care of the religious community is to be extended to all persons at all ages and that such care should include in particular the care of persons with special needs—the sick, the widowed and orphaned, the aged and infirm. Pastoral care, defined by the Judeo-Christian tradition, in the often quoted phrase of Seward Hiltner, as "tender and solicitous concern for the welfare of individuals" thus conjoins a general principle of attention to the needs of all and a particular principle of special attention to persons who are suffering or in pain.

Exactly how those two principles have shaped the praxis of the religious community and its ordained representatives at a particular time and place in relation to the general and specialized needs of the aging has varied considerably over the course of time. A cursory reading of the historical literature of pastoral care would suggest the likelihood that that variation has had primarily to do not so much with changes in interpretation of scriptural norms that govern the meaning of "tender and solicitous concern" as it has had to do with changing cultural patterns of interpretation with regard to aging itself. Thus, if I may risk an oversimplification, in historical periods

---

Charles V. Gerkin is Professor of Pastoral Psychology, Candler School of Theology, Emory University.

83

and cultural locations where aging persons were valued highly for their wisdom and longevity, that valuing tended to shape both the way in which the general principle of care of all aging persons was carried out and the way in which the suffering of the aging was given ministering response. In more recent times and cultural contexts like that of middle-class, upwardly mobile white America in the latter half of the twentieth century, the general principle of care of all aging persons has received a substantially different quality of attention than in earlier times and the manner of pastoral care for the sufferings of the aging has tended to be shaped to a considerable degree by current cultural images of the suffering that aging entails.

This assertion about changing styles of care for aging persons needs to be qualified somewhat by a recognition that consistently through the ages of the Judeo-Christian era there has been a common recognition that aging involves an inevitable degree of human pain. Since the writer of Ecclesiastes expressed the sad wisdom, "Remember also your Creator in the days of your youth, before the evil days come, and the years draw nigh, when you will say, 'I have no pleasure in them . . . ,'" there has been a consistent cultural understanding that with aging comes inevitable suffering. But the understanding of the suffering and the nature of the appropriate pastoral response to the suffering has been substantially different in varying cultural and time locations.

All that I have said thus far has been meant as an introduction to the theme that I want to pursue throughout the remainder of this presentation concerning pastoral care of the aging. Those of you who are familiar with my pastoral theological work will recognize it as a theme that I have been pursuing for some time in relation to a general theory for pastoral care and counseling. Stated briefly in relation to our present concern with aging, it is that the problem of structuring pastoral care for the aging, whether that be the caring relationship of the pastor with aging persons or the pastoral ministry of the congregation to and on behalf of the aging involves at a very practical level a hermeneutical task, a task of interpretation. Furthermore, the interpretive task has to do not only with interpretations of the meaning of pastoral care, but, perhaps just as or even more crucially, with interpretive models applied to the aging process itself. How the church and the pastor are to interpret aging as a human experience will set a pastoral and church ministry agenda. What we as pastors and congregations do will be in large part an outgrowth of what we see the process of aging to entail, in short, on the complex of interpreted meanings we and our aging parishioners attach to the aging process.

It is not my purpose, nor do I think it appropriate to suggest that there can be only "Christian" interpretations of aging. As a matter of fact, it is important to recognize that the Christian tradition and its sacred scriptures themselves evidence a certain pluralism of interpretive models with regard to aging. But it is also important to recognize that the model of interpretation applied, whether that application is undertaken self-consciously or by default, will be highly determinative of the care given. Rather than proposing a particular model as normative for Christian pastoral care I will first proceed to describe briefly several models that are currently popular in America and then propose an alternative model rooted in a contemporary theme in Christian theology.

THE SYMMETRICAL MODEL

I have adopted the term "symmetrical" for this model from the psychologist, Paul Pruyser. In an article that originally was prepared as a presentation to a major symposium on Theology and Aging sponsored by the National Retired Teachers Association and the American Association of Retired Persons in 1974, Pruyser presents this model as the primary one that has informed Western society's understanding of the aging process.[1] It is a model based on the image of life as "a peak between two valleys" or a process of development toward "fullness of life," followed inevitably by diminishment toward senility and death. In my pastoral care crisis ministry text, *Crisis Experience in Modern Life*, I schematized this model.

Within this schema, when rationally and objectively conceived, the anticipated normal life cycle will appear somewhat like a convex lens with the points of the lens signifying the beginning and ending points of birth and death. During childhood and adolescence the horizons of life are rapidly widening. This is the period of becoming, of growing, of expansion. Adolescence continues that process of growth, though the physical growth begins to diminish toward the end of the teen-age years. Adulthood is the time of full expression of human life and full responsibility for the affairs of the human world. Then comes the menopausal period, often referred to as "the change of life." From that point on the physical body begins to decline or contract in its capacities. It is probably important to recognize that the expansion of human responsibilities and creative cultural expression has tended, with the coming of civilization and certainly with the coming of modernity, to continue to expand beyond the physical menopausal time. Thus the schema proposes a human desire for the continuation and even expansion of human powers that is psychologically very powerful. But the reality of diminishment of powers and decline of physical body is inexorable as the organism moves toward aging and eventually death.

This schema proposes that a central psychological experience of aging is what is here called "anguish." That term is a useful one within this model because its root meanings have connections with both anger and entry into a narrowing place. In a sense it thus communicates the angry entry into the inevitability of aging. It also suggests that there is a fundamental contradiction in the human experience of aging—the slow realization of diminishment and the continuing strong desire for both longevity and expansion of lived experience.

If this "symmetrical" interpretive model is understood as the primary model by which aging is to be interpreted, certain understandings tend to be so normative as to be taken for granted. For most persons, at least those who experience the "fullness" of adult life as pleasurable and satisfying, the goals tend quite naturally to become the prolongation of this fullness of engagement of life for as long as possible. Youthful vigor must be maintained. Busy engrossment with the duties and responsibilities of life must be sustained at whatever cost. To "let down" is to acknowledge aging and thereby admit that one may be "over the hill," as we sometimes say. Aging becomes the hidden fault or the subtle and seldom acknowledged enemy within that must be refused, even denied, for as long as possible and grudgingly admitted to one's self or one's intimates largely in secret until it can no longer be denied. Meanwhile it may be spoken of in the terms of an ironic joke on oneself—a joke that both expresses and conceals the sense of defeat that aging interpreted as the enemy within inevitably brings.

Efforts must be made to ease the blows that inevitably come to the self's need to feel fully in charge and, as we often put it, "on top of things." The confrontation with narrowing limits on physical capacities is received as a blow to the narcissistic self—what is sometimes referred to by self psychologists as a "narcissistic injury." With aging there come with increasing frequency experiences that jar, even injure one's sense of control of one's life. Aging thus becomes what is often the greatest test of narcissism. Skills, mastery of life, powers to do significant things, all aspects of living that provide a sense of well-being, begin to diminish. Not only that, but the relationships that have provided intimacy and a sense of being of worth to others may become depleted and lost. All these experiences can be deeply injurious to the human psyche.

For those who have experienced the responsibilities of full adult life as burdensome or onerous and oppressive, on the other hand, there may develop a certain anticipation of retirement "when I will be free to do whatever I want to do." Aging becomes the anticipation of freedom that sustains a narcissistic sense of control of one's own destiny.

There is thus in the symmetrical model of aging a central image of life's progression as involving tragedy or existential limit. There is also the image of aging as fundamentally involving adaptation to a reality that stands over against human desires, hopes, and expectations. The "comedy" of life belongs to youth; its "tragedy" belongs to old age.

It is perhaps important to recognize the extent to which this model of aging both informs and is informed by much of both popular and more sophisticated inquiry concerning the "human life cycle" in our time. The image of a cycle of life from birth to death that is repeated from generation to generation is, of course, as old as human history. But because of a complex set of broad cultural developments ranging from the increasing dominance of a naturalistic, scientific mind-set to the diminishment of popular notions about life after death the cultural preoccupation with the human life cycle (often referred to in popular literature as the "biological clock") has developed apace in the last half of the twentieth century.

Just as the symmetrical interpretive model sets an agenda of issues and dilemmas for the aging person, so also it tends to set an agenda of prioritizing concerns for pastoral care of the aging. With the central image of aging as tragedy and coming to terms with existential limits comes the interpretation of pastoral care (as indeed all so-called "help" for the aging) as the process of assisting persons to accept the onset of limitations and adapt to the realities of the life cycle. Pastoral care becomes the art and science of assisting persons to adapt to the realities of the aging process. Pastors are to develop supportive relationships that facilitate adaptation to aging in a variety of significant ways, the variation dependent on the particularity of individuals and their situations. Pastoral care is thus directed toward supporting the continuation of whatever generative, creative capacities the person may possess in ways that adapt to the reality of diminishing resources over time. Pastoral care is also directed toward assisting persons to come to terms with the losses that inevitably occur, the anguish of the aging process. From this perspective pastoral care ministry with the aging has a certain affinity to ministry to the bereaved. It is in many situations a ministry of "grief work" in relation to the losses that occur, the injuries to self-esteem that are experienced by the aging.

There are important connections to be made here with the deep tradition of pastoral care within the Christian community. In the terms of that deep tradition, ministry to the aging within the symmetrical interpretive model may be seen as a form of the ministry of "sustaining." This, according to the classic nomenclature of pastoral care, is one of the four functions of pastoral care throughout Christian history. The others include the functions of guidance, healing, and reconciliation.

During these early centuries of the Christian tradition, pastoral sustaining took form in a fourfold task of helping persons troubled by an overwhelming sense of loss. The first task of *preservation* sought to maintain the troubled person's situation with as little loss as possible. Second, this function offered the *consolation* that actual losses could not nullify the person's opportunity to achieve his [sic] destiny under God. Third, *consolidation* of the remaining resources available to the sufferer built a platform from which to face up to a deprived life. Finally came *redemption*, by embracing the loss and by setting out to achieve whatever historical fulfillment might be wrested from life in the face of irretrievable deprivation.[2]

An example of pastoral care of the aging from my own early ministry experience is perhaps illustrative of the particularity of the ministry of sustaining. I was serving as pastor of a mid-sized congregation in a county seat community in mid-America at the time. In that community there was a small institution dedicated to the care of aged women that had been established by the will of one of the community's prominent citizens several decades earlier. I had several parishioners who were residents of the home that I visited regularly, sometimes taking communion. Two of these women parishioners stand out in my memory.

Mrs. Brown was a widow in her late seventies who suffered from numerous minor physical complaints — complaints that were exacerbated by her feeling of having been abandoned by her children. She had no recognizable interests or activities of her own to sustain her. Rather she spent most of her days preoccupied with her body and its aches and pains. My visits to her were marked by her rehearsal of these complaints concerning her health and her neglect by her children. My pastoral relationship was characterized by two efforts to sustain her: my willingness to listen and my intention to interest her in activities in the home and the congregation. I tried to bring her some news of persons she knew in the church each time I came. I also arranged for her to be placed on the regular calling list of a group of lay visitors in the congregation. I made a point of asking her about people and events in the institutional setting to which she was confined.

None of these efforts seemed to make any substantial impact on the narrowly defined self-preoccupations of Mrs. Brown's life, though she did seem to appreciate the visits I and the lay visitors made. In a limited sense, her connection with the relationships and meanings we who visited her attempted to represent did sustain her. At least it sustained that connection within the limits she permitted. In retrospect, I find myself wondering what might have happened if I had made a stronger pastoral move to intervene between Mrs.

Brown and her children. Family systems theory (something I knew nothing about at that time) would suggest the possible value of arranging for a family conference or two in which the question of Mrs. Brown's sense of neglect and perhaps the family's impatience with Mrs. Brown's pitiful self-preoccupation might be aired. Be that as it may, the pastoral care ministry to Mrs. Brown seems clearly to be within the model of sustaining her in a situation that seemed inexorably to be moving toward greater diminishment and death.

I probably remember Mrs. Jones largely because she related to me and her situation in a manner that stood in stark contrast to Mrs. Brown. Even though she was some five years older than Mrs. Brown and in many ways more physically handicapped, Mrs. Jones was a person who made strong and sustained efforts to remain involved with the world around her. Her room was filled with books and plants she loved and tended. She read the newspaper regularly and listened faithfully to the evening news on her little radio. Our conversations largely had to do with the outside world — everything from world and national affairs to happenings in the life of the community and church. She had a telephone and maintained close relationships with a number of friends with whom she talked regularly. She did not complain a bit about her state of immobility, but usually ended those remarks with some comment of satisfaction that she still had a number of avenues of interaction with things in which she was interested.

Although in a sense I found my visits with Mrs. Jones sustaining to my own life, I did sense that the regularity of my appearances to talk for a while were very important in sustaining Mrs. Jones in her valiant efforts to remain engaged and active in her world. Her life was in certain ways lonely in that she had no family in the community. She deeply enjoyed a chance to converse and share ideas. Her lively spirit needed sustaining interaction. Again, in retrospect, I wonder if I could not have done more to assist Mrs. Jones in her efforts to keep her world from contracting. Her telephone could have been put to helpful use in the life of the congregation. Her social zeal could have been channeled into forms of advocacy of those values and concerns that she sustained. I perhaps was too much influenced by the cultural images of aging that taught me to see her primarily as a person with needs to be fulfilled by my ministry rather than as a talented person who had much to contribute to the life of the community despite her confining physical situation.

There are, to be sure, a number of strengths to be found in the symmetrical hermeneutical model of aging and the quality of pastoral care that emerges from it. Its insistence on the reality of the aging process, its openness to the shame, loss and grief experienced by the aging, and its sophisticated appropriation of current psychological models of aging as the completion of the life cycle provide both an agenda of issues to be tended and a set of pastoral observational tools to be applied in pastoral work. In a sense the weaknesses of the model are inherent in its strengths: its tendency toward acceptance of culturally defined values in relation to the relative worth of youth and vigor over aging and diminishment of powers, its emphasis on what are essentially negative or "confining," "narrowing" experiences, and its concomitant lack of an adequate model of transcendence. The risk of its realism for both aging person and pastoral care practitioner is that it can take on a quality of pessimism, as if aging means inescapably fighting a losing battle.

The pastoral theologian, K. Brynolf Lyon, makes a useful theological/ethical contribution to this interpretive model with his notion that the fundamental task of aging comes at what he calls the metaethical level. From this perspective:

Old age can only properly be understood . . . as following the primary period of integration of moral becoming. As a second characteristic of this perspective, then, we can say that the period of life following the primary generative period raises the issues of the meaningfulness of the particular formations one's moral becoming has taken. This does not mean, of course, that older adults necessarily walk around talking about their past jobs or their children all the time. In its deeper sense, it has to do with the meaning of who one has become in the context of such generative issues (and in the context of one's full developmental history) and whether that meaning is sustaining in the light of the losses, challenges, and changes that accompany older adulthood.[3]

Lyon goes on to propose that pastoral care with the aging involves two aspects: (1) Facilitating appropriate meaning-making with regard to the metaethical task. This may involve "an explicit reworking of conflicts, 'mythologizing,' or shoring up crumbling defenses" as the particular person may require. (2) Facilitating the building of a value-consensus within the community which encourages and sustains such appropriate meaning-making. He goes on to argue that this ultimately involves more than just the care of individuals or groups, but necessitates the engagement of public issues in relation to the aging.[4]

PRUYSER'S LOSS/COMPENSATION MODEL

In the article to which I referred earlier in adopting Paul Pruyser's "symmetrical" label for the most widely utilized interpretive model undergirding both contemporary understanding of aging and pastoral care of the aging in America, Pruyser proposes a significantly altered variation of that basic interpretive construct. He attempts to counter the fundamental tragedy and pessimism that the symmetrical model engenders with a loss/compensation model as a counter to the loss/acceptance of inevitability image of most appropriations of the symmetrical model. Pruyser proposes that aging, though it involves inevitable loss and the concomitant suffering losses entail, also brings certain compensations. Pruyser's psychological orientation causes him to describe these compensations in largely psychological terms, but they nevertheless are significant for pastoral care in that they provide important conceptual tools for assisting pastors in both reflecting on and working pastorally in situations in which the aging are experiencing existential losses and narcissistic injury.

A brief listing of Pruyser's six compensations of aging will suffice to convey the direction his effort to ameliorate the inevitable losses of aging takes.

1. He proposes a gradual discovery on the part of many older persons of some good and wholesome dependencies. The full flowering of adulthood is marked for most people by both the requirement to become more self-dependent and to take on responsibility for others (to whom we often refer as our "dependents"). The re-

lease from the weight of responsibility for children and a more or less heavy schedule of work responsibilities that aging most often involves begins a process of reversal of this situation. Parents begin to see how much they can receive from their children, not only in terms of physical acts (I recall here a recent time when one of my sons assisted me in doing a yard task too heavy for me to do by myself, for example), but even more in terms of their infusion of liveliness and acts of care and affection. Experiences begin to occur that cause the aging to reconsider in important ways their former strivings for independence.

2. Aging can bring the ability to redefine one's own status in more personal and less instrumental terms, thus relieving one from some of the hierarchies of status related to occupation, income, and social approval for being "in charge" or "on top of things," particularly in the working world. Having become who one is, one is no longer oppressed with the obligation of "making it," whatever that might mean in one's social group.

3. Pruyser speaks of a certain relaxation of psychological defenses. "With greater and more profound knowledge of the inevitable ambiguities of life and acceptance of irreducible ambivalence of one's own feelings, unpleasant realities can be faced with less denial, and negative affects or dubious propensities are no longer prone to lead to reaction formation."[5]

4. Aging, according to Pruyser, often brings a greater capacity to live in the present as distinct from always looking to the future. Oldsters "can enjoy more because they enjoy it now, in the present moment."[6] He goes on to suggest that for those who have religious faith, the faith that has sustained them in dark times in the past, sometimes defensively, can now become a more reflective and even enjoyable cosmology that "beautifies and validates their present days."

5. Pruyser proposes that the relief from the heavy responsibilities of the middle years of life can strengthen aging persons' capacity to identify with the idealism of youth and thus conjoin the hard won wisdom of years with a reappropriation of the ideals and values of the young. Here this hermeneutical model suggests a reawakening or reopening of life's possibilities as counter to the diminishments of the constrictions of aging. In subtle ways the model therefore

proposes the possibility of transformed styles of interaction with the world made possible by the same alterations of structures of relationship that the symmetrical model interprets as losses.

6. Finally, Pruyser suggests that one of the compensations of aging may be a new-found freedom to reveal one's innermost thoughts. "However honest and open a person may have been before, aging gives him [sic] new candor for speaking without inhibitions."[7]

Interpreting aging and pastoral care of the aging in the categories provided by the loss/compensation model will tend to a degree to ameliorate the tragic image of the symmetrical model and thereby modify somewhat the pastoral theological thrust of pastoral care from the traditional function of sustaining in the direction of pastoral guidance. Pastoral guidance has traditionally included as one of its purposes assisting persons in the making of choice decisions and in the redirection of their commitments and energies. It has likewise included the role of assisting persons to reexamine their relationships, whether that be relationship to self or to others. It has thus had at its core the image of facilitation of persons' strengths and exercise of free, if limited, choice rather than the image of sustaining persons who have suffered irretrievable losses. In this way a more positive, less negatively tragic note is introduced into the ethos of pastoral care of aging persons. The confrontation with reality becomes not simply tragic and constricting, although that may indeed be present, but also the confrontation with as yet unrealized possibilities.

ERIK ERIKSON'S EPIGENETIC MODEL

Erik Erikson's model of the life cycle is one that has been widely adopted as a psychological structure that informs pastoral care ministry to persons at various stages in the process of maturation and aging. Although Erikson's model can be seen as simply a variation of the "symmetrical" model of aging, it contains implicitly a somewhat different emphasis than the physical reality of development and diminishment that model is built upon. For Erikson the human life cycle cannot fully complete itself—arrive at its full development—until the last stage when what Erikson speaks of as integrity becomes a pervasive possibility. The achievement of the integrity of life's final stage involves, at least implicitly, a circling back to the first virtue of stage one in infancy, the virtue of trust. Trust and integrity, in the healthy senior citizen, are for Erikson conjoined. Thus rather than emphasizing the diminishment of aging, Erikson maintains an image of fulfillment and full-orbed realization of the goal of the entire life process as the achievement of healthy aging.

Aging within this hermeneutical model becomes the time that makes possible a perspective on the whole of life that is not fully possible until the "length of days" of a lifetime has taken place. Aging thus brings into focus a way of valuing all of human experience that both relativizes the person's sense of one's own life pilgrimage and affirms its unique worth. Thus Erikson's perspective points to a possible experience of transcendence that both accepts the limits of a single life and points beyond its boundaries toward values that transcend its limits in relation to the continuing cycle of the generations. In this way Erikson's model begins to press against the "expansion/diminishment" quality of the symmetrical model by means of its vision of wisdom and integrity growing out of the process of the life cycle as its fulfillment.

A HISTORICAL/ESCHATOLOGICAL MODEL

Building on all three of the models thus far discussed, yet going beyond them to embrace an explicit Christian theological narrative hermeneutical theme, I would propose the possibility of developing what I will call a historical/eschatological model that can shape both an interpretation of aging and of pastoral care of the aging. This is to suggest that aging be envisioned as a time that, in what appears to be a paradoxical fashion, marks the coming together of an individual's historical identity and his or her appropriation of a Christian eschatological identity.[8] Since it is not possible to develop fully the scope and pastoral implications of such a model in a short presentation such as this one, what follows should be taken as only suggestive.

This model would build upon the symmetrical model to acknowledge that a primary aspect of the aging process beyond mid-life does indeed have to do with coming to terms with the reality that we humans are finite, historical creatures who have the privilege and gift of being present in creation as we know it only for the limited span of a life cycle. Coming to terms with that is both a confrontation with limits — the limits of *my* finitude — and an opportunity to find new and compensatory value in the attainment of the long look of history, i.e., a sense of one's history that Erik Erikson is reaching for in his concept of epigenesis and its goal of ego integrity. But the sense of history made possible by aging is not only that pertaining to one's own historical experience. It is in a real sense the opportunity to "place" one's self within human history and, as Erikson suggests, to achieve the integrity and singularity that goes with that.

Aging, however, presents also the possibility of seeing the limits of historical life as it has been in human history and as it is presently known to the person as being contained within a larger and more open-ended vision of the future God is bringing about — in theological language, the eschatological vision of God's future. Historical self-limits thus come up against the limitlessness of God's eschatological future.

Said another way, the thrust of this interpretive model has to do with a relocating of the ground and basis of hope for the aging from the arenas of "hopes" for the self's future to the arena of participation in the great hope of humankind found in the Christian eschatological vision. In the Christian tradition this shift from human life "hopes" toward a larger vision of Christian hope has very often taken the form of a variation on the ancient mind/body dualism. The pastoral theologian, K. B. Lyon, reminds us that the way aging has been seen as offering possibilities of "growth" has often involved the notion that, as the body declines, there become available new opportunities for "spiritual growth." The spirit of the aged, now less encumbered by the "passions of the flesh," is left free to focus on spiritual growth. There is an implicit contrast here between the transient and the permanent — things that pass away and things that are permanent. "Nature is subject to the cycle of growth and decay (thus the decline of our physical being with aging), while spirit (when rightly related to God) may continually 'advance in newness of life.'"[9]

Lyon goes on to contend that this dualism cannot be sustained either on the basis of modern thought or biblically. Modern pastoral care theory has generally been psychologically supported by an understanding of the human as being a unity of body and spirit. Yet, he says, there is much in the contemporary pastoral care literature that still sees the dualism as the principal position to be overcome. In popular culture the passions are often seen as inappropriate "sins of the flesh" in the aging.

It is probably important, if one is to take the eschatological hope tack on the problem, that it be kept in some degree of tension with the "aging as decline of powers" model in order that there be some taking into account of the inevitable losses and decline of physical abilities that come with aging. Here the image of human identity as paradoxically historical and eschatological developed by Jurgen Moltmann and further elaborated in my *The Living Human Document* is perhaps most apt. An aspect of what Moltmann calls our human historical embeddedness involves our embeddedness in the physical realities of the life cycle with its progression toward old age and death. Eschatological hope and eschatological identity therefore are always in a tension with the reality that we are finite, historical creatures.

Such a sense of one's own life and all of human life as being contained in the limitless life of God moves, of course, beyond what Erikson envisions in his emphasis on the embracing of the cycle of generations on the part of aging persons. Working within the confines of human categories, Erikson sees the fulfillment of aging as arising out of the accomplishment of the generative tasks of adulthood. Integrity in the aging is therefore the outcome of fulfilled generative responsibility for the coming generations. Eschatological identity, however, is not finally dependent upon human generative accomplishment, important as that is, but rather rests on the confidence of faith in the promises of God with regard to the future of all things. The self's integrity is stitched into the integrity of God's future which is both open-ended and limitless.

The historical/eschatological model of aging likewise builds upon but moves beyond the loss/compensation model suggested by Paul Pruyser. Like that model, it suggests that the attainment of advanced stages of aging brings with it not only experiences of loss, most particularly the loss of physical powers, but also certain valuable compensations that can enhance the person's sense of freedom from many of the real and imagined burdens of life. The primary compensation, however, made available by the historical/eschatological interpretive possibility has to do with the enlarged and less humanly dependent context within which one's total life and present situation can be understood. Not only does aging bring the possibility, as Pruyser suggests, of learning to enjoy and value certain human dependencies; within this model it also brings the possibility of "enjoying" and "valuing" the final dependency of human life, human hopes, and human expectations on the ongoing life of God. Aging interpreted within the historical/eschatological paradigm is thus aging "in God," in the phrase of Jurgen Moltmann.[10] By allowing one's own life and history to be placed within that context the aging persons can be set free from not only the psychological defensiveness to which Pruyser points, but also the need to "defend" one's life span as of ultimate importance within itself. The eschatological context thus can enable a freeing of the self of the aging persons to live within the enlarged context of God's promise and future.

To be sure, it is both unnecessary and unrealistic to propose that all aging persons should or could envision their own life span and its limits within the specific language symbols I have here used to suggest the historical/eschatological model. The actual language symbols, indeed the experiential meanings which might provide the vessels for such an experience of aging, must needs come from the images and themes that make meaningful connection with the individual life in question. But the tone and direction of appropriation of the aging process the model embodies may in a rich variety of ways be possible for many aging persons if the relational context can be provided that facilitates it.

A model of pastoral care with the aging is thus suggested by the historical/eschatological model of aging about which I have spoken only in very general terms. Put very simply, the model of pastoral care it suggests will be governed by the intention to facilitate in whatever way possible the experiencing of the aging process by persons receiving the care of the church and its ministers from within the historical/eschatological interpretive model of aging. The historical/eschatological model is thus proposed as both normative for church and ministry pastoral practice and inclusive of most of the descriptive elements of the other three models.

Engaging the task of pastoral ministry with the aging from within a historical/eschatological model for pastoral care of the aging can undergird in significant ways the facilitation and, on occasion, the physical provision of both interpersonal and institutional/communal contexts of human interaction and care where aging persons may experience their aging from within the historical/eschatological model of interpretation. This involves two distinct but interacting processes, the facilitation of the self-interpretation of aging on the part of aging individuals and the interpretive ethos that surrounds aging persons and interprets aging for and to them. With regard to the first, those providing pastoral care will seek to relate to the aging in ways that invite their coming to self-understandings that incorporate the values and meanings of the historical/eschatological model. The model thus provides for the development of pastoral relationships with the aging that invite reflection, sharing of the experiences of loss associated with aging, and search for new and transformed self-understandings that incorporate the values of the historical/eschatological model. Here all of what was discussed earlier concerning pastoral appropriation of the symmetrical, loss/compensation, and Eriksonian epigenetic models becomes significant. The pastoral response to the shared search of aging persons for new self-understanding will, however, be guided by the core meanings of the historical/eschatological model.

With regard to the second socio-cultural interpretive context, the church and its ministers will engage in whatever social, political, and missional activities are appropriate to seek the transformation of societal attitudes toward aging in the direction of the values directly contained or implicit within the historical/eschatological model. The church will both seek to enact and embody those values and meanings in the institutional and missional programs it sponsors and advocate those values and meanings in the public arenas that affect the care of the aging. The model thus will seek to conjoin traditionally pastoral/priestly modes of ministry with prophetic/missional modes of congregational engagement of societal issues.

The thesis of this essay has been that the experiential content, issues and dilemmas, as well as the outcomes of both aging itself and pastoral care of the aging are to a considerable degree dependent upon the interpretive model governing the operational understanding of aging and pastoral care as response to aging. Three interpretive models receiving attention in contemporary theories of aging have been examined and a fourth theologically grounded model has been briefly proposed. Further theoretical work needs to be done to bring these four models fully into mutually critical correlation, particularly in relation to the many and varied specific problems of pastoral care of the aging in American culture. The practical application of the model likewise deserves further elaboration. The possibilities for both individual and societal transformation with regard to aging embodied in the model have however, even from a brief comparative study such as that undertaken in this short essay, revealed themselves to be highly suggestive for pastoral practice.

NOTES

1. Paul W. Pruyser, "Aging: Downward, Upward, or Forward" in Seward Hiltner, (Ed.), *Toward a Theology of Aging*. (New York: Human Sciences Press), 1975, pp. 102-118.
2. William A. Clebsch and Charles R. Jaekle, *Pastoral Care in Historical Perspective*. (Englewood Cliffs, New Jersey: Prentice-Hall), 1964, p. 43.
3. K. Brynolf Lyon, *Toward a Practical Theology of Aging*. (Philadelphia: Fortress Press), 1985, p. 77.
4. Ibid., p. 83, 84.
5. Pruyser, op. cit., p. 114.
6. Ibid.
7. Ibid., p. 116.
8. Charles V. Gerkin, *The Living Human Document*. (Nashville: Abingdon Press), 1984, p. 67. See also Jurgen Moltmann, *The Church in the Power of the Spirit*. (New York: Harper & Row), 1977, p. 192.
9. Lyon, op. cit., p. 59.
10. Jurgen Moltmann, *The Crucified God*. (New York: Harper & Row), 1974, pp. 252-255.

Christian Education and Older Persons in Congregations

Edward A. Trimmer, EdD
Betsy Styles, GCG

SUMMARY. A review of the relation of various aspects of Christian Education to the needs of older persons in congregations. This is followed by practical suggestions for planning programs for and with the elderly.

CHRISTIAN EDUCATION AND THE ELDERLY: EDWARD A. TRIMMER

What is the nature and purpose of Christian Education in the local congregational setting? This question has many answers at the present time in American "mainline" Christendom.[1] How a congregation answers this question will determine to a significant degree the educational ministry of the church. This especially holds true for the church's educational ministry which is developed in relationship to those considered old, elderly, or retired. Since there are several different understandings of Christian Education, this paper will not argue for the primacy of any specific one, but will examine from several differing perspectives, the implications for an educational ministry with the elderly in a local church.[2] The term "elderly" will refer to those 65 years of age and over.[3]

Traditionally, many churches have followed the schooling paradigm of the general culture as they sought to implement their educational ministries. This schooling paradigm has focused almost ex-

---

Edward A. Trimmer is Professor of Christian Education, Columbia Theological Seminary. Betsy Styles is Executive Director of the Northside Shepherd Center, Atlanta, Georgia.

clusively on the young, assuming that these were the persons who needed education and who could be educated. Conversely, the assumption seemed to be that the elderly were too old to learn or didn't need to learn. Obviously, these assumptions have limited a congregation's educational ministry to/with the elderly in the congregation. These attitudes must be overcome if churches are to have a truly effective educational ministry with the elderly. There are myriad concerns that can be addressed by a traditional schooling paradigm, not the least of which are what Henry Simmons has called education for retirement and leisure, education for loss, and education for social and theological critique.[4]

Recently the culture in general and "mainline" churches in particular have re-discovered spirituality. This has led to an increasing number of persons identifying spirituality, the search to know God, as the purpose of Christian Education. In such settings an educational ministry of spiritual formation and discipleship would involve helping the elderly to understand their particular faith journey, to share their faith stories with intergenerational groups within the faith community, and to continue to grow in their particular faith journey. Thus for some, spiritual direction for the elderly would be the primary focus of Christian Education.

Another way of thinking about the purpose and nature of Christian Education is in terms of goal-setting, planning, executing, and evaluating. Determining the needs of the elderly through working with them, planning ways to meet those needs with them, executing the plan and then evaluating the results — this would be the methodology which this understanding of Christian Education would employ.[5] This methodology has great potential if we remember to work with the elderly. They need to be part of the process from the beginning.

Another way of thinking about Christian Education is that it must be grounded and take its focus from theology.[6] Were this to be the case the educational ministry would need to focus on some of the theological issues that arise out of particular life experiences of the elderly. A list of theological issues ought to be determined by the elderly themselves.

Another way to focus the educational ministry of a congregation is around the concept of a "faith community."[7] Here it is important that the whole congregation gather to worship and to learn together. The idea of segregating people by age or even interest is not supported. Rather, more emphasis is placed upon bringing the whole people of God together to worship and learn from each other. This would obviously mean a great focus on intergenerational events and learning situations. The mingling of faith stories of all the generations together would be another important facet of this understanding of Christian Education.

While these differing ways of looking at the educational ministry of a congregation do not exhaust the debate on the nature and purpose of Christian Education, they do illustrate differing ways of thinking about it.[8] These brief comments may provoke images of how a congregation might respond to older persons. They provide some guidelines for any congregational response to educational ministry to/with/by older adults. Obviously assumptions about the nature and purpose of Christian Education guide these thoughts.[9] These are:

1. An educational ministry ought to be intentional. Each congregation needs intentionally to focus and think about their educational ministry with/to the elderly.
2. An educational ministry ought to include persons of all age groupings in visioning, planning, implementing and evaluating stages.
3. An educational ministry ought to serve as an advocate for the elderly. It should seek to affirm the elderly, change societal structures that deny that affirmation, and encourage leadership by the elderly. Thus, social and denominational policies that affect older adults ought to be scrutinized and addressed.
4. An educational ministry to/with the elderly ought to be free from barriers of participation including those barriers that are created because of vision, hearing or physical access issues.
5. An educational ministry to/with the elderly ought to be both a ministry *with* the elderly and *to* the elderly. The elderly need to be involved in all aspects of the ministry. Further it must not be assumed that the elderly cannot be in ministry themselves. Thus the elderly must be challenged as well as given the opportunity to be in ministry.

6. An educational ministry with/to the elderly ought to serve as an advocate for participation of the elderly in the total life of the congregation including worship life.
7. An educational ministry to/with the elderly ought to provide opportunities for the continuing personal growth of the elderly, including spiritual growth.
8. An educational ministry to/with the elderly ought to be intergenerational, providing opportunities for all ages of the faith community to gather and learn from one another.
9. An educational ministry to/with the elderly will challenge the elderly to continue to be faithful to God and use their gifts and talents in appropriate ways.
10. An educational ministry with/to the elderly will address those deep theological issues that arise out of aging people's life experience such as the purpose for living and death.
11. An educational ministry to/with the elderly will be aware of the organizations in society that serve the elderly and will help the elderly to have access to and understanding of those services. They will not develop programs for an educational ministry in isolation.
12. An educational ministry to/with the elderly ought to foster a better understanding and awareness of aging and older people in the entire congregation and culture.
13. An educational ministry with/to the elderly ought to provide care and support to the elderly during times of transition and personal distress as well as reaching out to those isolated by illness, frailty, or loss of loved ones.

It may be difficult, in the beginning, to rethink and reshape the church's educational ministry with/to the elderly. Certainly the curriculum issue has not been addressed in any substantial way at the present time. Additionally, the sense of the purpose of life being either to work or to have fun is fairly pervasive in our present culture. This makes it difficult for the elderly to deal with the loss of work and the loss of physical health (which may limit one's ability to have fun or be happy). The church has the means to address these issues. The church understands the purposes of life (to oversimplify) as doing justice, loving kindness and walking humbly with one's God (Micah 6:8). One can do this at any age, in any span of development. As the church ought to be serving both those within and without the church walls, it is called to address the issues raised by an aging church and an aging society. The educational ministry of the congregation is just one place where the church needs to rethink and reshape its ministry to an aging church and culture. Yet with God's help and direction, we can begin and continue to be faithful in our ministry in general and our educational ministry to/ with the elderly in particular.

CONGREGATIONAL PROGRAMMING FOR OLDER ADULTS: BETSY STYLES

This section considers some of the elements in developing programs in congregations with aging membership.

Defining the Older Adult

Programing for older adults at the congregational level involves an understanding of the stages of adulthood and life events, lifestyle changes, transitions and losses. Social changes resulting from technology, urbanization and the sexual revolution have affected the timing of many adult life events so that it is difficult to put a chronological age on them. We are out of timing with many major life events such as age of first marriage, the birth of the first child, retirement, when we die and how. This confusion of life events becomes even more complex when we attempt to decide who are the older adults in our congregations.

Chronological age, even when we decide on one, is difficult to determine in many congregations because the age is not a part of most membership records. If not age, how do we identify the older adult? How can we plan for older adults until we define the group? One way is to use a time line of older adulthood like the one suggested in Figure 1.[10] What life events mark the social entrance into older adulthood? What changes make an adult realize he/she has entered a different phase of adulthood?

Is it retirement? The age of eligibility for full social security ben-

Figure 1. TIME LINE FOR OLDER ADULTHOOD

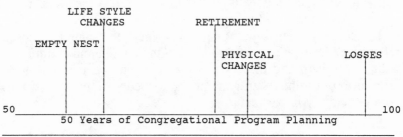

Adapted from Thomas Robb, Unpublished Lecture, 1987

efits has become the social definition of retirement. Contrary to this popular usage, the trend has been toward early retirement. This has been particularly true in the 1980s as corporate America has bought out early retirement for a sizeable number of persons with 20-25 years of service. Retirement is becoming an unexpected mid-life event for many. Mid-life is becoming the ending of one career and the beginning of a second career. There are many examples of the second career being the more successful such as that of Gray Panther founder Maggie Kuhn. Retirement as the definition of an older adult is debatable.

Is it lifestyle changes? Permanent retirement at any age may lead to a change in lifestyle due to income and/or the need to change residence. It may be due to widowhood or divorce.

Is it the "empty nest"? Is one an older adult when the last child leaves home? The question in the 1980s is, do children really leave home? Recent research shows that single adult children are leaving the "nest" much later and there is a trend toward "returning" to the nest with grandchildren for older adults to parent.

Is it losses? These could be linked to lifestyle changes such as loss of status due to retirement, loss of income, loss of work network, loss of friends and family due to moving or death, loss of physical functioning, loss of sexual potency? These lifetime losses become cumulative.

Is it physical changes? The appearance of the first gray hair or wrinkle followed by other physical appearance changes may be visual images for identifying an older adult. Sometimes it is a functional limitation brought about by disease and/or chronic illnesses. For most adults, it is the first glasses indicating some loss of vision. Later there may be some hearing loss. Any of these changes could occur at any age. The fact is, they seem to be cumulative in the older stages of life. However, these changes do not happen to everyone. If and when they do occur, they do so at different ages and throughout the older adulthood period.

What age can we use for the beginning and ending of the time line? If a specific age is used to begin the time line of older adulthood, what is it? 50? 62? 65? 70? Some, like the American Association of Retired Persons (AARP), use 50 years of *age* as the beginning of older age. Others use 62, the age of partial eligibility for social security. The most frequently used age is 65 because it marks eligibility to receive full social security benefits. What was set by law is by law changing. By 2027 it will be 67. There are exceptions to the law abolishing mandatory retirement. In October 1986, the Age Discrimination in Employment Act was amended to prohibit job discrimination at any *age*. Some organizations are using a younger, some an older age as the social indicator of entrance into older adulthood. Since AARP has more than 28 million members and uses the earliest age of 50, it is most inclusive to use it to mark the beginning of the time line. Now the question is, at what age does the time line end?

One way to visualize the end of the time line is the decline or lower end of a bell curve. The end of life for the Christian is a double line: A descending line for the physical aspects and an ascending one for the spiritual. Death as the end of life at any age is the ascending life line for the Christian who believes in the resurrection. The ascending spiritual growth that never is ended by a birthday or a retirement event is the core or foundation for congregational programing.

What is the age at the end of the time line? The average life expectancy at birth in the United States is 74.4 but for women it is 7.5 more years. The most important new improvement in life expectancy now affects those aged 65 and over. In the United States a male aged 65 may expect 12.8 more years and a female 15.8 years. Old is getting older and the differences in life expectancy at every age by gender increases with age.[11]

The fastest growing age group in American society is the over 85 years of age and, in that group 210 adults reach the age of 100 every week![12] Given these data, we are adopting 50 years of age as the beginning of the older adulthood time line and 100 years of age for the end. Congregations have fifty years of church programing to plan with and for older adults. Many in the over 50 years of age group were infants at the same time other older adults were experiencing mid-life crisis. Discounting the differences related to birth cohort, older adults are the most heterogenous group in the population. This compounds the problems of program planning. However, in any given congregation, the older adults (however identified) can be expected to have more commonalities than those of their same age group in society. Planners do need to avoid stereotypes within the older adult group and avoid locking them into frisky, frail, and fragile categories or the "go-go's," "go-slow's," "no-go's" and the "won't go's." Older adults tend to move in and out of these depending on the life events they are experiencing.

Some categories of life that are useful for program planners have been developed by Tobin and Lawson as shown in Figure 2.

What's in a Name?

What do we call this person who has entered the older adulthood stage? The elderly, as in an elder in the congregation, aged, old folks, senior citizens, mature adult, senior adult? Research indicates that "senior citizen" has been more acceptable to the over 50 group, but is losing popularity. The Baptist denominational literature and church school organization has adopted the term, "senior

Figure 2.   Categories for Program Planners by Lawson and Tobin

LAWSON [13]		TOBIN [14]	
Group 1:	healthy, active	Group 1:	Well elderly
Group 2:	less active, slowed down physically	Group 2:	Homebound
Group 3:	Homebound, recuperative limited	Group 3:	Nursing home residents
Group 4:	Institutionalized: temporary or permanent	Group 4:	Dying

adult." "Older adult" has been used by the Methodists since 1950. What we know about names is that very few adults in America in the older adulthood stage want to be classified by any name. A rose by any other name is not so sweet in planning for older persons. From all the designations, we have chosen to use "older adults." It is most likely that the name game will continue until youth worship and the stigma of being old is destroyed. For planners this is a caution to be careful about the name of a group or activity. The very title may interfere with full participation.

The Planning Process

The planning process begins with a review of the items listed above to determine intention and attitudes. The bottom line for beginning is that programing should be by/for/with older adults. From planning to implementation and evaluation it should include older adults with the support of the leadership of the congregation.

The goal of the planning is to empower older adults to assume or reclaim control of their own lives. Empowerment fosters the independence of the older adult by building upon personal and community resources.

Prior to establishing a permanent committee, it is recommended that a task force be selected from congregational leaders. Such a group has a limited time period to accomplish specific tasks for the new program. The task force should include such persons as: (1) natural older adult leaders such as older adult Sunday School presidents, (2) presidents of men's and women's groups, (3) older adult volunteers in the church (receptionists, newsletter/bulletin collators, visitors, records keepers), (4) a representative from any older adult group meeting in the church such as AARP chapter, an ecumenical group such as a Shepherd's Center,[15] and (5) the pastor and a staff person. It is important that the clergy and staff see their role as enablers and facilitators and that leadership be in the hands of older adults. The end result should be a program in which older adults have ownership from the beginning.

At the first meeting of the task force, it should be stressed that it has a short time frame for its existence, such as the implementation of the first program. Most likely the task force will become the nucleus of the leadership for a permanent committee or organization. Task force members need to remember that this is an emergent process which requires flexibility and is most likely to have drop-adds in leadership.

Each task force member usually has his/her own agenda about programs. Yet, the task force's job is to find out what are the needs of the older adults and what are the resources of the congregation to meet these needs. The only way to do this is to *ask*. At this point, the task force's work is to outline its first plan of action and how to achieve it. This calls for a needs assessment survey.[16]

Needs Assessment Survey

To design the survey of the congregational needs among the older adults and congregational resources, there are several essential factors to address:

1. Support of the congregational leadership. The congregation must be convinced that the survey is critical in the planning of the older adult program. This task begins with the senior clergyperson and extends to the lay leadership of the congregation.
2. The purpose of the survey. A clear and action oriented statement is needed to present to the leadership and to include in the survey. This statement informs the leadership of what the survey will accomplish.
3. The survey should elicit information about the needs of the older adults, the resources and skills of the older adults, their willingness to be volunteers, and the services older adults would like to see developed.

The task force must decide on the type of information needed and how much they want to gather. The survey instrument evolves from those decisions. Examples of surveys may be found in the program organization books such as those by Kerr,[17] Clingan,[18] Senek and Anderson,[19] and others.[20] They vary from simple 3 × 5 cards to several pages and may be adapted for use by the task force. A pre-test of the survey on a few older adults provides valuable feedback for revision and could be vital to a successful survey.

The next step is to decide how to administer the survey. The most successful method is the personal interview. It also requires more time and trained interviewers. The mailed survey takes less volunteer time, but usually results in less information. With the mailed survey the task force needs a plan for encouraging returns such as notices in church bulletins and newsletters about the reason for the survey, support from the pulpit, and announcements in the various congregational groups. In addition to these public efforts, the task force should have a follow-up plan for collection of the surveys. The greater the number of completed surveys, the greater the amount of information upon which the task force can base their programing decisions.

The results of the survey become the basis for determining the start-up program and date. Publishing the results of the survey will be informative to the congregation and will generate more interest in the first program.

The survey and prioritizing of specific programs are the beginning steps of the planning cycle (Kerr,[21] Lawson,[22] and Clingan[23]). The next steps involve: (1) locating the resources to support the program such as skilled persons, facilities, materials, and funding. (2) Meetings. At times progress seems slow and requires many meetings. Going slowly and being thorough about the first program will most likely insure a strong foundation not only for the start-up program, but for future programs. (3) Evaluation should be built into the program. Evaluation models (Bergman and Otte[24]) may be adapted for use with the new program. The feedback from the participants is invaluable in determining the direction of the program and/or developing additional programs. The evaluation may also serve as a survey of needs from the participants that may vary or change the prioritizing of the congregational survey.

By the time the start-up program is under way, the task force's time is up. It may become the nucleus of the older adult program committee or council.

The winner in the planning process is the older adult. This strategy matches the older adult as a resourceful leader with the needs of the older adults in the congregation. With ownership in planning older adults strengthen the effectiveness of the congregation's program in this area.

NOTES

1. The definition I understand of "mainline" is the one that Roof and McKinney have put forward in their work *American Mainline Religion*. Rutgers: Rutgers University Press, 1987. "By mainline we mean the dominant, culturally established faiths held by the majority of Americans."

2. If readers would like to explore this issue in more depth they can do so by reading Thomas Groome's work, *Christian Religious Education*. San Francisco: Harper & Row, 1980. See Chapters two and four of *The Religious Education of Older Adults* by Linda Jane Vogel, Birmingham, AL: Religious Education Press, 1984.

3. The author is well aware that one cannot generalize "elderly" into one developmental age span with similar characteristics. Even a definition of the young-old ages 65-75; the middle-old ages 75-85, and the old-old ages 85 + is a gross generalization.

4. Henry Simmons is primary author of "Religious Education" in *Aging Society: A Challenge to Theological Education* published by the American Association of Retired Persons, 1988. Dr. Simmons is not crystal clear on what he means by the term, "education for retirement and leisure." It is clear that he is not referring to "educational programs for retirement and leisure that are little more than financial planning seminars or appeals to self-control, nutrition, exercise, volunteerism, and good health as appropriate ways of staving off the vicissitudes of age" (p. 38). By "education for loss" he appears to be referring to helping people deal with all the various kinds of loss that one encounters as one ages. By "education for social and theological critique" he appears to be advocating that the elderly rise up from the oppression of society and find a way to have personal meaning in their lives.

5. This particular methodology is very well established in the minds of many local church educators. David Ng explores this issue in his piece entitled "The Church's Educational Ministry with the Aging" in the Austin Seminary Bulletin, October, 1980.

6. This particular argument has taken many forms. Currently its most popular form is either basing Christian Education on the tenets of Liberation Theology or in locating Christian Education in the developing debate around Practical Theology.

7. Ellis Nelson's Book *Where Faith Begins*, Atlanta: John Knox Press, and some of John Westerhoff's works such as *Will Our Children Have Faith?*, New York: Seabury Press, 1976 illustrate this type of approach.

8. Certainly the debate around whether conversion or nurture is the purpose of Christian Education is not new nor has it been resolved. For many in the more "conservative" churches and denominations there is no debate: the purpose of Christian Education is conversion, and the Sunday School in particular is the entry point into the church. However, in many "mainline" churches the debate is still active or has been resolved in the favor of "nurture."

9. This particular topic, aging and what the church can do is "in" at the present time. Thus denominations such as the United Methodist Church are creat-

ing older adult programing agencies, and programing-type materials are being published by various persons and companies. I have found two works to be helpful for this general understanding: *Affirmative Aging: A Resource for Ministry by Episcopal Society for Ministry on Aging*, Winston Press, and *Older Adults Ministry: A Resource for Program Development*, Presbyterian Publishing House.

10. T. Robb. Unpublished Lecture. Georgia State University, March, 1987.

11. B. B. Torrey, K. Kinsella & C. M. Tauber. *An Aging World: International Population Report*, Series P-95, No.78. Washington, DC: Bureau of the Census, 1987.

12. Robb, op. cit.

13. R. J. Lawson. *Our Congregation's Ministries With Older Adults*. Nashville: Discipleship Resources, 1983.

14. S. Tobin, J. W. Ellor & S. Anderson-Ray. *Enabling the Elderly: Religious Institutions Within the Community Service System*. New York: New York State University Press, 1986.

15. The Shepherd's Center is an ecumenical program based on the original 1972 Kansas City project. The general goal of the Shepherd's Centers is to "sustain older people in their homes and engage them in meaningful activities which give purpose to life." The older people participate in the planning and operation of the Center. More specifically, the objectives are: (1) to sustain the desire for independence characteristic of most elderly people, (2) to offer an integrative approach in meeting individual needs by bringing a wide variety of services from one center, (3) to focus on the elderly of a specific geographical area, small enough to accomplish the goals of the Center, (4) to provide opportunities for the elderly to serve and engage in meaningful activities, (5) to avoid isolating the elderly from the rest of the community, (6) to develop a model which could be duplicated elsewhere in the city and in other communities, (7) to make more effective use of existing community resources and programs designed to help those 65 and over. B. P. Payne, "Voluntary Association of the Elderly." Unpublished paper presented to the Society for the Scientific Study of Social Problems, August 27, 1973, Warwick Hotel, New York, NY.

16. M. Bergman & E. Otte, *Engaging the Aging in Ministry*. St. Louis, MO: Concordia Press, 1981.

17. H. L. Kerr. *How to Minister to Senior Adults in Your Church*. Nashville: Broadman Press, 1980.

18. D. F. Clingan. *Aging Persons in the Community of Faith* (Revised Edition). Indianapolis, IN: The Indiana Commission on Aging, 1980.

19. F. J. Schenk & J. V. Anderson. *Aging Together, Serving Together*. Minneapolis, MN: Augsburg Publishing House, 1982.

20. *Older Adult Ministry: A Resource for Program Development*. Atlanta, GA: Presbyterian Publishing House, 1987. A loose-leaf guide for program development designed to help develop ministries by and with older adults.

21. Kerr, op. cit.

22. Lawson, op. cit.

23. Clingan, op. cit.

24. Bergman & Otte, op. cit.

Worship and Gerontology

Melva Wilson Costen, PhD

SUMMARY. Worship and liturgy are reviewed in terms of the life and faith journeys of older persons. Various norms for evaluating worship are proposed: biblical, theological, historical, psychological, sociocultural and ecclesiastical.

The matter of time, both *chronos* and *kairos*, is important to chronicles of God's intervention in human history. The Creation story recorded in Genesis sets God's time (*kairos*) "in the beginning" (Genesis 1:1). Events are set forth and identified by particular times: "And there was evening and there was morning, a fourth day" (Genesis 1:19) ". . . a fifth day" (1:23) ". . . a sixth day" (1:31), "and by the seventh day God completed God's work" (2:2). The story of God's intervention in human history is recorded in Genesis with such references as ". . . it came about in the course of time . . ." (4:3) and continues with many references to age, aged and ages. Abraham and Sarah, in their "old age" became the parents of a son, thus, human history acknowledges the fruitfulness of the aging, albeit in this instance highlighting procreation.

It is of interest that in the Book of Ruth the birth of Ruth's firstborn evokes a concern for the sustenance of the aging. The women in this story bless God for the gift of the son of Ruth and Boaz including these powerful words addressed to Naomi: ". . . May he be to you a restorer of life and a sustainer of your old age" (Ruth 4:15).

From another perspective, the Psalmist, in speaking of life as transient and futile, cries before the Lord, "Behold, You have

Melva Wilson Costen is Helman Nielson Professor of Worship and Music at the Interdenominational Theological Center.

made my days as handbreadths, and my lifetime (age) as nothing in Your sight'' (Psalm 39:5). The handbreadth, a measure only four fingers wide, implies that life is worthless compared to God's love. As one ages, sustenance should be granted, and regardless of age, human life is as a shadow which quickly passes.

Perhaps the natural flow of time and aging prevented the recorders of biblical history from underscoring the need to recognize the direct concern for the aging in preparing liturgy. Recently, however, liturgical scholars remind us that liturgy reflects the journey of life. William Oden is quite specific in his observation that:

> Liturgy is the community's life-journey. Its sole purpose is to make visible the presence of Christ at each point of existence-birth, coming of age, family style (married and single), times of despair and times of ecstacy, times of growing and times of standing still, youth and old age, death as the completion of life and trust in God beyond death.[1]

Soren Kierkegaard suggested earlier that worship is in itself to be understood as drama with God, rather than the congregation, as the audience.[2] As drama, liturgy includes the whole worship setting: God, the initiator, as well as the congregation with their needs and expectations. Viewed holistically, liturgy should express the journey of particular congregations which come both with uniqueness and commonalities in all times and places. The story of God's people begins with remembrance and a retelling of particular life-journeys of faith (and non-faith) of those who have gone before. Liturgy is also a symbolic process through which this story becomes "our story." A particular story must reach persons on a level through which they may respond but must also stretch and pull them beyond where they are at any particular moment.

Denominational statistics indicate that a large percentage of congregations today reflect memberships which are middle-aged and over. Those of us involved in revising and developing new hymnals for the church are reminded through responses on questionnaires that they should be inclusive of "old hymns/songs of the faith" reflective of a generation which needs familiar language. These data sufficiently affirm the need for serious concern for the aging.

The word "liturgy" which is used here synonymously with worship, comes from the Greek word, leitourgia, meaning "the work of the people." In the early Christian era, leitourgia was used to describe the common worship of the gathered church. Members of the community created the liturgy to retell the story of Christ and to rehearse the meaning of their lives reflective of the new life in Christ. Liturgy-worship was and continues to be the central manner in which the church expresses its nature, its ethics and mission. The major "work of the people" is to live out the "work of Christ," therefore, liturgy both reflects and expresses life. Under the power of the Holy Spirit the person and the community are empowered to witness to Christ, who is the embodiment of the redeeming Word. Worship is a channel connecting Christ's sacrifice on our behalf and our thankful response. At the core of liturgy is always the outpouring of thanksgiving (Eucharist) for Christ and his redeeming and unending love. Through praise, prayer, preaching and the sacraments (ordinances) the community becomes one with God in Christ, one with the whole family of the early faithful and one with each other.

For liturgy to be authentic, then, it must serve as a guide to the entire pilgrimage of faith. Only liturgy that is authentic, meeting the needs of all ages, will reflect these intersections, or as Dag Hammarskjold called them, "Markings," on the spiritual journey, where the Gospel meets life. Crises will be noted and interpreted, events will be acknowledged, and Christian nurture will take place. One of the means of marking points along the journey is through the celebration and interpretation of the Christian church. As events in the life of Christ are retold consistently, the human faith journey will have more meaning.

Liturgy should also provide opportunities for assurance of acceptance by God and the community at all stages of life. By definition liturgy is communal, so that all of the congregants are affirmed by virtue of their being a part of the Body of Christ. There is no single event in the life of the Christian church which surpasses the potential inherent in worship. Thor Hall is quite correct in his observation that the service of worship is the "one event that is still the plenary session of the people of God."[3] When liturgy is unrelated to the whole life of the people of God, unity in Christ and in the lives of persons, the Word of God is being fragmented by those who profess to be faithful. Herein lies one of the essential factors in a discussion of worship and gerontology: through baptism one enters into a life which implies communality with the divine Godhead lived in unity with all the faithful.

AGING: AN INTEGRAL ASPECT
OF THE JOURNEY OF LIFE

Baptism by water is an important rite of passage which marks the beginning of a life-long pilgrimage. It signifies arrival and a process of going. Theologically, Baptism is a gift from God to humanity in which Christ, present and active, "seals" the baptizand to himself and admits the faithful into the fellowship of the church. Through the visible sign of baptizing, Christ "demands" that the recipient respond in faith and in action, through the power of the Holy Spirit. In the waters of Baptism the sign of pledge of God's saving grace is made. This sign, along with the bread and wine of the Eucharist (Lord's Supper) puts humanity in touch with the archetypical story of the universe. It recalls the original saving event of God's work for us and our incorporation into the ecclesial family. With an understanding of Baptism, one should recognize how we are part of a whole sequence of events forming the social transition from birth through life to death.

During the first phase of the journey one identifies with those who have also accepted the mystery of grace and salvation. The first response is to become Christ's disciple as one lives in the midst of a world that may not always appear to understand what it means "to follow." The journey includes a return to "the Holy moment of incorporation" at each service of worship, as others are Baptized, during the Lord's Supper, at each opportunity to nurture others, and as he/she is continually nurtured. Nurturing implies growth both spiritually and physically. Thus, the journey continues as one ages chronologically and spiritually.

Worship as a gerontological phenomenon, therefore, is rooted in Christian Baptism. While specific concerns were not always identified by the term "gerontology," the theology of worship shaped in the earliest centuries recognized the life journey of humans which it shapes. In their concern for fulfilling the call for persons to edify and nurture each other, church leaders always turned to worship. Paul enthusiastically reminded the First Church at Corinth that Christian worship is primarily an arena to strengthen the community (I Cor. 1:2; 14:26). Karl Barth reminded the church that: "It is not only in worship that the community is edified and edifies itself. But it is here first that this continuously takes place. And if it does not take place here, it does not take place anywhere."[4] William H. Willimon aptly states that ". . . in worship, all the community's concerns meet and coalesce . . . Here word and deed, theoria and praxis, past and present, humanity and divinity meet."[5]

Perhaps it is not by accident that Christ gathered individuals into a body of believers, redefined the table meals, and that the Spirit broke into differences and integrated diverse races and nations at Pentecost, all of which imply the kind of worship life that we must live. Worship should indeed be a synaxis, a coming together, as the early shapers of worship indicated. The young, the aging, and the aged are inclusive of Christ's Body gathered for worship.

All worship services can be evaluated according to certain norms which are applicable across denominational lines. Included are norms which are biblical, theological, psychological, sociocultural, historical, and ecclesiastical, all of which have pastoral dimensions. The needs and concerns of the aged are covered in these norms, if indeed, worship is to be authentic and have integrity. It is important, therefore, that planners and executors of worship (pastors and liturgists) understand each norm, and utilize pastoral skill in ministering to the needs of all of the people of God.

Biblical Norm

The whole word of God, according to scripture, must be preached and heard by all. Care should be taken to ascertain biblical truths as services are planned. This includes not only that which is preached from the pulpit but all elements in the order of service must be grounded in scripture. Recognizing that there is no prescribed order in scriptural sources, this necessitates clarity about how the biblical message is communicated in the ordering and carrying out of elements in the service. Central to every service of worship is the Word of God. Nothing should detract from this fact!

Theological Norm

The basic questions asked in the evaluation of this norm are two-fold: (1) What does our worship/liturgy say about God? (2) What does God say to us about our worship? These questions would help us avoid the one most often asked: What did I get out of worship? This question emerges because people have come to worship. To be theologically concerned allows us to keep our minds attuned to the voice of God, rather than on our personal needs. This is not to say that we should leave our needs at the doorstep of the church, for we worship as whole persons. Unfortunately, many contemporary services seek to satisfy persons as if humans rather than God should be praised.

Paul might have had this in mind when he admonished the young church at Corinth to avoid selfish indulgences (in eating the sacred meal) when they gathered (I Cor. 11:29). There is a need to recover some of the mystery inherent in worship. The theological norm reminds us that why and whom we worship are infinitely more important than how much there is in it for an individual!

Historical Norm

In worship we affirm the various ways that our foreparents in faith spoke and listened to God as part of the continuing relevance for us today. We can learn much from the biblical record about the need for reform. The prophets cried out against faithlessness and overemphasis on sacrificial offerings evidenced in worship. The historical shape of the liturgy during the Medieval Era also became stagnated under the guise of order. Martin Luther and other reformers recalled for us the need to return to biblical events for models, and to recognize that liturgy is in constant need of reforming. There is truth in the axiom that those who do not know their history are subject to repeat the mistakes of history. Equally true is the fact that past history can help in shaping positive directions for the present and future.

Psychological Norm

If worship is to be viewed holistically, the whole person must be taken into consideration in planning. Worship provides an arena where psychological needs are met in the presence of and under the guidance of the Holy Spirit. Persons bring to worship a number of needs that can be divinely met: a sense of mystery which seeks an opportunity for probing and understanding; a sense of finiteness which searches for the infinite in the divine; a sense of insecurity which seeks a place of security and refuge; a sense of loneliness which seeks companionship with the Almighty; a hunger for human belongingness that can be satisfied in mutual fellowship with others; a sense of guilt and anxiety which longs for forgiveness and peace; a sense of fear that seeks assurance in the community of faith; a sense of brokenness which longs for healing; a sense of meaninglessness which longs for fulfillment and purpose; and a sense of grief over loss—any loss—which needs to be comforted.

In each of the above areas we can find persons of any and every age, but particularly those who are aging and willing to admit that certain needs are prevalent. The pastoral concern here is also obvious. Where there are those who are not willing or able to articulate these needs, a pastor can help persons own and express them with the assurance that God is constantly concerned.

Sociocultural Norm

Worship is very much shaped by and within sociological and cultural contexts. This is evidenced both biblically and more specifically historically. As the faith is transmitted to groups of people, worship styles, rather than being adopted in toto from a particular people, are forged in the light of the contextual experience of the recipients of the faith. Christians in Third World countries, for instance, would bring their particular gifts as they lift up their voices in praise and adoration to Almighty God. Afro-Americans heard the gospel message through their African heritage and shaped new forms of worship in the light of their existential situations. These new forms are often defined as "simply emotional" without acknowledging that the worship arena is often the only arena where "marginal" people can be free to praise God as the author and only source of liberation and love.

The growing population of aging Christians are anxious to shape the liturgy in keeping with their life journeys. The pastoral concern in this regard, should be obvious. A new shape is likely to occur within local congregations in the light of the extended life journeys richly present in their midst. What a tremendous opportunity to hear the Word of God through the lives and voices of those with experience!

Ecclesiastical Norm

The liturgy always reflects a particular denomination's historical shaping. Pastors are prepared in seminaries to lead congregations from the standpoint of denominational doctrines. These should clearly be kept in mind as worship is planned and executed. There are various sacramental theologies which are experienced in worship and from which theologies of worship evolve. Care should be taken that these are observed.

An area of concern which can be highlighted by pastors is the elderly. Most denominations are aware of this special area of concern, often with little happening about it. Pastors are, or should be, encouraged to become change agents within their denominations to facilitate and urge a recognition of the aging. This is not only a suggestion but an obligation as the aging population increases.

THE ROLE OF THE NEW GENERATION
OF PASTORS WITH THE AGING

The concept of gerontology is notably an African concept where "government or rule by the elders" is not only understood but also valued. Although the term itself has Greek and French roots (from the Greek "geron" meaning "old man"; and the French "geronto"), the high respect for the wisdom of the aged in Africa granted them the power to rule the people. Much can be learned from this and any group as it recognizes the extreme value of those whom God blesses with long life journeys.

The role of the new generation of pastors, as the writer sees it, is to learn from history, both that recorded in the Bible as well as the history of cultures where persons of all ages are respected. All ministers, clergy and lay, should become well versed in the knowledge of liturgical history from biblical roots through the socioculture contexts of their worshiping communities. Only then will the importance of worship in life journeys have meaning. Only then will ordering of worship reflect both the kairos and chronos in divine order.

Combined with liturgical knowledge should be the knowledge of gerontology and geriatrics. The present age is replete with possibilities for pastors to take seriously life journeys in human and divine history. God has called us to such a time and we should be willing to respond in keeping with our own life journeys.

NOTES

1. William B. Oden, *Liturgy as Life-Journey*. (Los Angeles: Acton House), 1976, p. 5.

2. Soren Kierkegaard, *Purity of Heart is to Will One Thing*. (New York: Harper and Brothers, Torchback Edition), 1956, p. 181.

3. Thor Hall, *The Future Shape of Preaching*. (Philadelphia: Fortress Press), 1971, pp. 38-39.

4. Karl Barth, *Church Dogmatics*. Trans. G. W. Bromiley, IV/2 (Edinburgh: T & T Clark), 1958, p. 638.

5. William H. Willimon, *Worship as Pastoral Care*. (Nashville: Abingdon Press), 1979, p. 20.

Spirituality and the Later Years

Ben C. Johnson, PhD

SUMMARY. Three questions are raised and discussed. What is the meaning of spirituality? How is spirituality affected by the aging process? And what are some suggestions for spiritual ministry to the aging?

WHAT IS THE MEANING OF SPIRITUALITY?

In defining spirituality I will begin with a generic definition suggested by Urban Holmes:

> Spirituality is a human capacity for relationship with that which transcends sense phenomena; this relationship is perceived by the subject as an expanded or heightened consciousness independent of the subject's efforts, given substance in the historical setting, and exhibits itself in creative action in the world.[1]

This definition suggests a comprehensive view of the experience of transcendence. The essential structure of spirituality is a relationship between an experiencing subject and a reality which transcends sense phenomena. The effect of this encounter on the experiencing subject is a heightened or expanded consciousness—a deepened awareness of self, other, and world. But this spiritual experience does not take place in the consciousness alone; it is given substance in the historical setting, that is, it draws upon the data of the person's life for its shape and substance. Finally, spirituality is not primarily for the maturity of the individual or the healing of the

Ben C. Johnson is Professor of Evangelism and Church Growth, Columbia Theological Seminary.

brokenness of a personal life; a deepened awareness of the Holy must exhibit itself in a creative action in the world.

This definition of spirituality suggests a matrix within which spirituality develops. The matrix for a developing spirituality is the God/self relation — the initiatives of God and the response of the persons. Holmes refers to this dyadic structure as the "human capacity for relationship with that which transcends sense phenomena . . ."

The context for a growing spirituality refers to that web of relations which a person has with her or his world. The geographical location, the particular network of relations on a job, the political commitments which one may have and the family in which one lives — these illustrate what I mean by context. Holmes suggests that these relationships in the "real" world give substance to one's spirituality.

Since Holmes offers a generic definition, one that provides a phenomenological description of spirituality, he does not include the specifically Christian dimension. Spirituality from the Christian perspective must include a relation with fellow believers in the Christian community. The inclusion of community in the shaping of spirituality suggests the role of Word and Sacrament, rituals, traditions, and symbols in the nurturing of one's relation with the Transcendent.

For our purposes time is a crucial element in spirituality. Time always dictates the questions that humans ask about God. If you think of Erik Erikson's eight stages, for example, the questions of the adolescent are quite different from those of the person in generativity. Similarly, the experience which one has of God is, or should be, different in these different stages of life. "Different" refers to experience, not to God. Time provides a critical aspect. Time not only dictates the questions but makes the answering of those questions most urgent.

Destiny refers to "that which one was meant to be." John Sanford, following his mentor, Carl Jung, says, "There is something within you that knows who you are and what you are supposed to be." The "something" refers to destiny which is written into the structure of one's being. This aspect of the matrix relates to the struggle of Erikson's eighth stage, the struggle to see that one's life has fulfilled its purpose.

Holmes begins his definition with "the human capacity." This human capacity refers to human consciousness, awareness. All persons have awareness; they are and they know that they are. To say "I am" requires the powers to stand outside the self and look upon that self as one object among many; in other words, persons are "self-transcendent." In the power of self-transcendence, the subject encounters mystery—the mystery of his or her own being and meaning.

Human beings have the capacity to transcend themselves in the direction of the past. They can recall yesterday, the day before, last year, and so on until they arrive at the origin of their personal being. They not only can recall the experiences of their lives but, thrust up against their origin, can even imagine the time when they were not. At their point of beginning they encounter an awareness of the mystery which stands behind their being.

Who of us has not asked, "Where did I come from?" This question thrusts us against the ground, the origin, of our being. The question is itself a spiritual question, the foundational question in our search for meaning.

Another existential question involves transcending oneself in the present, either consciously or unconsciously. "Who am I?" is the question of identity which stems from participating in and interacting with one's community of origin. "Where do I fit in? What is my place?" As the question of identity arises in the present, it introduces yet another question each person asks. "Why am I here? What am I to do with my life?"

Humans also have the power to transcend themselves in the direction of the future. In the power of a creative imagination, we can imagine the sun rising tomorrow, the fruits of old age, and death. Humans can and do picture a time when they will be no longer. And the question forces itself upon human consciousness, "Where am I going when I die?" Again, this question presses consciousness hard against the mystery which surrounds us.

This human capacity to ask the existential questions of meaning stands at the center of the spiritual matrix described earlier. These questions are questions of being and meaning. According to Peter

Berger in *The Sacred Canopy*, the human craving for meaning seems "to have the force of instinct." Berger insists that humans "cannot accept meaninglessness."

In the face of the mystery encountered through these questions, humans are driven to faith. H. Richard Niebuhr writes, "as long as a man lives, he must believe in something for the sake of which he lives; without belief in something that makes life worth living man cannot exist."[2] The capacity to place one's trust in and give one's loyalty to something of transcendent meaning and value is faith.

But what is that for which one must live? What is the name we give to that which claims our trust and loyalty? Again Niebuhr: "Man as a practical, living being never exists without a god or gods; some things there are to which he must cling as the sources and goals of his activity, the centers of value."[3]

So what is the human situation? Unrequested, humans find themselves thrust into mystery. In the power of their creaturely self-transcendence they can ask questions about origin, identity, purpose, and destiny. From the center of their being, they are driven by a demand for meaning which has the force of instinct from which they cannot escape. This search for meaning has a focus; and this center is the god or gods which provide power and value.

Then what do humans do? They construct stories from the experiences which they have as interpreted by the world in which they live and the gods they worship. The story which they tell carries the meaning of their lives. As we look at this narrative from the latter years of life, we not only find meaning, identity, and perspective in the story, but we, in fact, continue to refine the story so that it speaks our destiny.

If the reader is asking, "What has this power of self-transcendence, the search for meaning, loyalty, and narrative to do with spirituality?" I answer, "It is the person's spirituality." Spirituality in persons is the form which that instinctual search for meaning takes. There are several forms of this spirituality.

1. Evangelical piety is a form of spirituality found in conservative churches with a Puritan or revivalistic tradition. In evangelical spirituality persons encounter God through the word of God. By reading the scriptures, understanding the authoritative message,

discerning the will of God, and doing the will of God, persons experience true and vital spirituality.

Normally this type of piety expresses itself in personal witness to others, in speech punctuated with references to God or the Holy Spirit with an aim toward conversion or edification of the hearer. Generally this has clear guidelines for living the Christian life.

This piety develops "in the closet," that is, it grows through a daily discipline which is set aside for prayer and the reading of the scriptures. It includes meditation on the scriptures, fasting, and days of prayer.

Evangelical piety has a strong appeal to the sensate, extroverted type who enjoys reading the scriptures, praying, and witnessing, and who likes to have things spelled out in black and white.

The strengths of this style come from its intentionality to build on the biblical revelation. It creates a passionate people willing to work and sacrifice for Jesus Christ. The commitment to make God's will a priority is admirable. Both devotion and sacrifice of self and money are to be commended as an authentic expression of Christian commitment.

The weaknesses of evangelical piety stem from its tendency toward legalism. It may also become judgmental. Sometimes the form of spirituality remains after the life of the Spirit has gone out of the form.

2. Charismatic spirituality has a kinship with evangelical piety in the seriousness of its devotion. It is found in Pentecostal and neo-Pentecostal congregations and is scattered throughout mainline denominations, especially among Episcopalians and Roman Catholics. Charismatic spirituality is associated with the gift of the Holy Spirit and the Spirit's present activity in the Body of Christ. God is met in the experience of the immediate presence of the Spirit. The Bible mediates this experience, but the experience is also drawn from groups, praise services, and charismatic worship.

Charismatic piety expresses itself in the charismatic group through a demonstration of the gifts of the Spirit. Some groups demand that believers speak in tongues as evidence of possessing the Holy Spirit. Charismatics often have an "insider" way of speaking which sets off their identity.

The charismatic also reads the word of God and prays. In private devotions the devotee may use a prayer language known as "speaking in tongues." This form of spirituality finds support in a group or community which shares the experience and practices the gifts.

Charismatic piety appeals to the intuitive, feeling type. These persons feel the depths of their devotion to Christ. Most will tend to be extroverted rather than introverted in a demonstration of the gifts.

The strength of charismatic spirituality is found in the immediate experience of God. Those in the fellowship who have been touched by God also have a depth of dedication, making them willing to risk and sacrifice for the sake of the gospel of Christ.

The weaknesses in charismatic spirituality stem from its emphasis on intuition, feeling, and experience to the neglect of intellectual substance. Like other forms of spirituality, there may also be imitations of the true gift of the Spirit. Frequently, this spirituality is other-worldly, with little concern for social transformation. In the worst case, charismatic spirituality lacks a deep self-awareness, an ignorance which the devotees seek to cover over with religious experience. In this latter form, it often covers personality deficiencies and defends against painful growth.

3. Sacramental spirituality contrasts markedly with charismatic spirituality, though they may become compatible. Sacramental piety is found predominantly among Roman Catholics, Greek Orthodox, and Episcopalians. The presence of God in sacramental spirituality is mediated through the sacraments. In eating the bread and drinking the wine, the worshiper encounters the real presence. Liturgical prayers and the celebration of the church year are other sources of mediation.

Sacramental piety expresses itself in a sacramental life. The liturgy of worship, the church year, festivals and celebrations provide the structure of sacramental piety. The world of nature is viewed sacramentally and mediates the presence of God; history also contributes as the unfolding of God's story.

The setting for strengthening sacramental spirituality is worship, especially public worship. It is further strengthened through the prayer book, private bidding prayer, and spiritual reading.

Sacramental spirituality appeals to the sensate, thinking type. This spirituality has a "thereness" about it which gives it objectivity when feelings dry up. The liturgy gives structure but also creates a space for thought and reflection.

The strength of this form of spirituality is its objectivity in the sacraments. The sacraments are valid despite the inauthenticity or lack of awareness within the worshiper. This spirituality orders life and gives stability to life in the face of the abyss of non-being. A sacramental view of nature and history gives a certain "at home-ness" to life in the world.

One danger of sacramental spirituality is a dependency upon ritual which can become empty. When the liturgy becomes merely rehearsal, the worshiper leaves the sanctuary empty and hollow. This form of spirituality often fails to emphasize personal disciplines and radical discipleship. It tends to favor corporate spiritual formation over personal spiritual formation.

4. The activist meets God in social service and political action. This piety is found predominantly in the left wing of mainline denominations or in secular form in issue-oriented groups like the peace, anti-nuclear, and ecology movements.

For the activist, God is not to be found primarily in the church or in religious practices, but in the world. God is already at work in the world, and the activist meets God by joining God in what God is doing in the world.

An activist spirituality expresses itself in action. It aims to function in solidarity with God in specific social transformation. This form of devotion reacts against a private, cloistered, passive piety.

The activist finds renewed energy and motivation from grasping a new issue, serving on a task force, challenging the establishment, and protesting the status quo. The activist also draws strength from others involved in the mission.

An activist piety appeals to an extroverted, intuitive feeling type. These persons make a difference in the world. They feel deeply about causes and possess high ideals. Even though they may not know how to reach their goals, they are willing to sacrifice both themselves and their resources in an effort to change the present order of life. Change is a dominant motive for the activists.

Perhaps the weakness of this approach, as commendable as it may be, comes from its lack of spiritual depth. It often loses the awareness of God in the action which purports to be a manifestation of the will of God. When this occurs, action degenerates into works of righteousness and human effort. Disillusionment follows. Cynicism is the ripened fruit of disillusionment. Burn out occurs, paralyzing the once brave disciple. The value of this approach is its relevance and ethical commitment. It aims to change the real world. It defines spirituality in terms of the kingdom of God and gives concrete expression to a vision of transformation.

5. Academic spirituality is the opposite of activist piety. To some persons academics and piety present contradictory images. In the popular mind piety appeals to feeling over intellect. But those persons who think about God and systematize their thought express relationship with God through the mind. Probably the most outstanding example is St. Thomas Aquinas, who wrote the *Summa Theological* and in the end was given a beatific vision of God.

This piety is found in scholars, theologians, teachers, and studious clergy and consists of research and thoughtful reflection. This was the piety not only of Aquinas, but of other contemporary theologians and scholars. For the academic, the encounter with God is mediated through rational thought. Research results in a system which relates the truth of God to life; a deep awareness of God occurs through thought. This style of spirituality expresses itself in a lifestyle of study, careful analysis of issues, reflection, and teaching. When the system is completed, the academic feels fulfilled. This piety finds strength and reinforcement in the academy. It may express itself in reading, occasional papers, discussion of insights with a discerning mind, and writing books.

Academic piety has the strongest appeal to an introverted, intuitive, thinking type. These persons tackle complex issues and seek to know and understand reality. They are less concerned with sharing their insights with others than are the extroverted types.

The weakness of academic piety may be found in its frequent loss of a reverence for the Holy through its intense focus on the data of theology or the specific issues being addressed. It can become cold and impersonal. The scholar may have an answer but may also have little passion for involvement in life. This form of spirituality, though valuable, may end in cynicism.

The strength of academic spirituality is its ruthless pursuit of truth; it faces the issues of life boldly and honestly. This spirituality will move in new directions as the truth demands. It resists a weak sentimentalism or a shallow, superficial emotionalism.

6. Ascetic spirituality is found in monastic orders among priests and nuns. In its Protestant form it appears in world-denying holiness movements. Some lay persons may also be ascetic in discipline and practice. Ignatius, for example, formed the third order of laity who were married and engaged in the practical affairs of life but lived out the monastic ideal in the world.

For the ascetic, God is met in the daily office, spiritual literature, and mental prayer. The ascetic lives a life of contemplation and self-denial as an expression of devotion to God. The lifestyle of the ascetic is that of prayer, rest, and work in the cloistered society of the monastery. Simplicity is the key to the ascetic life. This ascetic form of spirituality is reinforced by the three-fold view of poverty, chastity, and obedience.

This type of piety will appeal to introverted, sensate types. Their introversion enables them to endure the silence and solitude; their sensate ability enables them to be oriented to the facts of the outer world.

There are some dangers in the ascetic approach. It can become an escape from the world, though not necessarily. It requires a rigid discipline which denies certain aspects of humanity. Its routine can also become deadly and lose its meaning. Monastics are not exempt from emptiness or dryness of soul.

This style has a clear, corporate discipline which orders life and gives it support. In its best form, it is an unselfish offering of one's life in prayer for the world. It demands a life of simplicity and studied concentration on God.

7. Eastern spirituality is found in Buddhistic groups in which a union with God is sought. In this approach to piety the seeker usually pictures God as part of the self; to get in touch with the self is to get in touch with God. Transcendence is within the person.

The religious experience of the East manifests itself in peace. This often results in a withdrawal from the world. The goal is the loss of the self and the cessation of desire. This experience can be strengthened by a disciplined practice of meditation, fasting, and solitude. Though meditation may be a group practice, it tends toward a strong individualism.

Those persons who are introverted, feeling types will find this approach most compatible with their temperament. Other persons with thinking as a dominant function may achieve this union with the All but with greater effort.

The strength of this type of piety is its demand for control over the body and its appetites; it offers welcome relief from active engagement for rushed souls. Perhaps its weakness from a Christian perspective comes from a lack of interest in history, the welfare of individual persons, and passionate involvement in the world.

8. A review of the forms of piety just described suggests the necessity of forming a wholistic understanding of spirituality which grows on the strengths of the seven forms and seeks to avoid the weaknesses identified in each. The following affirmations point toward a wholistic piety.

A wholistic piety must be connected to the Church, the Body of Christ, a community of worship. The main setting will be in the corporate community, but scheduled times alone for private worship are important. The presence of God comes through the external events of history and nature, human intelligence, theology, the Bible, and Christian tradition. The presence of God also comes to consciousness through the under world of intuition and imagination. Genuine piety must express itself in a simplified, Christ-centered life of love. Life can be enriched through periods of silence and keeping open to the inner depths of the Spirit.

Personal spirituality will be reinforced through personal and corporate worship and through daily meditation on scripture or some other spiritual writing. Regular retreats, plus the sacraments, will enrich one's sense of God's presence. Spirituality must search for a balance between extroversion and introversion, sensation and intuition, thinking and feeling.

In summary, a wholistic spirituality recognizes the importance of the biblical norms of an evangelical piety; the freedom of the spirit to impact human consciousness immediately, as the charismatic affirms; sacramental piety's emphasis on the sacramental nature of life and the ordering of life in a sacred way; the necessity for engagement with real needs and the issues of persons as found in activist piety; the necessity of developing the intellect as emphasized by the academics; and the periodic retreat for personal denial and self-examination as demonstrated by the ascetics. This style of spirituality seems wholistic, balanced, corporate, and personal.

SPIRITUALITY AND THE LATER YEARS

Now we raise the question of the influence of aging on a maturing spirituality. Our approach will be to examine aging with the help of Paul Maves (*Faith for the Older Years*) and Erik Erikson (*Vital Involvement in Old Age*). It will be helpful to look at aging in stages, to identify some of the changes which it incurs, and to suggest a few appropriate spiritual tasks.

Paul Maves writes, "I prefer to think of later maturity as the last one-third of our lives."[4] Age 55-64 is a time of preparation; 65-74, years of activity; 75-85 and beyond, years of loss and diminishing activity.

Maves points to meaning as one of the dominant themes for the latter stages of life. "So to think about the process of aging is to raise the question of the meaning and purpose of the life which is loaned to us for a relatively brief span of years." He goes on to say that "The awareness of our own death . . . fuels the concern for the quality of life and how best to use the time we have."[5]

I have found in my mid-fifties a desire to look at the remainder of my life, to identify the things that are worth living for, and to refocus my energies for the last third of life. It is my intention to give this desire a specific focus for an extended period of time.

The transition into the later years introduces a series of new tasks. According to Maves, the retirement years call us to the following tasks:

1. to discover new sources of value for our lives;
2. to work out our worth not primarily through achievement or activity, we must find value in being;
3. to find new ways of structuring our time, new outlets for our energy;
4. to adapt to new environments—move to a new community, different home, different geographical setting;
5. to learn to be single again. During this period it is possible, even likely, that a spouse will die;

6. to cope with new physical limitations. These may come from illness, accident, natural deterioration.[6]

Maves says we must learn to say "Amen" to all of life. We have no viable choice but to accept and affirm the one and only life which is given to us. The later years introduce us to new tasks. Each of these has a depth dimension which is spiritual in nature. These tasks are to simplify our lives, accept what we are, heal the bitter memories, be a good steward of our health, reach out to others, find a reason for being, see life in the context of eternity and prepare to die.[7]

In *Childhood and Society*, Erikson sets forth his eight stages of psycho-social development. We will look primarily at the eighth stage, ego integrity versus despair, and its implications for a maturing spirituality. He identified several characteristics of ego integrity:

1. The accrued assurance of its proclivity for order and meaning.
2. A post-narcissistic love of the human ego — not of the self — as an experience which conveys some world order and spiritual sense.
3. Acceptance of one's only life cycle as something that had to be and that, by necessity, permitted no substitutions.
4. A new, different love of one's parents.
5. A readiness to defend the dignity of one's own lifestyle.
6. In such final consolidation, death loses its sting.[8]

The opposing force in the eighth stage is despair. Erikson describes despair this way: "Despair expresses the feeling that the time is now short, too short for the attempt to start another life and to try out alternate roads to integrity."[9]

Erikson's book, *Vital Involvement in Old Age* is a follow-up on the research done earlier. The source of information came from the records which had been kept on 248 families beginning in 1928-29. Every third child born in Berkeley, California, became a subject of this study. Records of interviews with the parents were kept through the child's eighteenth birthday. In 1981 the Eriksons and Helen Kivnick elected to interview the parents of the children who had been part of the original study. From them they felt they could gather information about old age since most were over 75 years of age.

Their interviews confirmed the following regarding those 29 parents who were still living and could be located. Some were struggling to accept the inalterability of the past and the unknowability of the future. They had found in parents and grandparents models for dealing with their own aging process. Most seemed to have an increased tolerance for differences between themselves and others. They had greater patience and were slower to become angry. Nothing shocked them anymore. Many recognized that they held views which were incompatible. They showed a greater tolerance for ambiguity. Most found themselves involuntarily thinking about dying. They tended to recall beliefs, rituals, experiences from church. Some returned to the church, especially in times of crisis. They tended to view their lives romantically; they did not recall the conflicts, pain, and unhappiness which they experienced earlier. They tended to gloss over what the records of earlier interviews actually contained.[10]

I propose that the virtues of the eight stages form the structure of spirituality. These virtues are: hope, will, purpose, competence, fidelity, love, care, and wisdom. It appears to me that the biblical view of spirituality seeks to form these virtues in believers. Each can be supported by scripture references.

From the first stage of life these virtues begin to develop; they are reworked in each stage; and, they come to maturity in the final stage. In the eighth stage, life weaves back upon itself, integrating in maturing forms the virtues which have been developed through the life cycle. Each of these virtues climaxes in the eighth stage. Wisdom represents mature care, a care which reaches beyond what one has created either in children or work; it includes a caring for the whole of God's creation.

In the final stage, love reaches its zenith as "unconditional positive regard" for all persons, races, and types; it is a universal love for the human family. The fulfillment of fidelity is the acceptance of one's only life; it is to have lived that life and to regard it positively in the unfolding scheme of history. Competence finds its fulfillment in having done what one was supposed to have done; to be reconciled with one's failures; and, in the end, to accept what one has accomplished. The maturity of purpose is the confidence that existence is not and will not be futile; there is purpose in life, in the cosmos and beyond time. The maturity of volition is to have exercised the freedom of one's own will, to have owned it as an autonomous self and, finally, to surrender one's will to the will of God. Hope, the fruit of trust, looks into the future with the confidence that one's life does belong to God and that the God who gave being has a place beyond time for this one and only personal life. This kind of maturity and confidence, it appears to me, cannot be achieved apart from the revelation of God in Jesus Christ.

SUGGESTIONS FOR SPIRITUAL MINISTRY TO THE AGING

The term "spiritual ministry" is not ideal, but it was the only way I could give emphasis to a ministry which focused on the spirituality of the later years. Here are some suggestions for this spiritual ministry.

Deal with your own fears about the elderly, your own aging and your own fear of death. Deal with your feelings of inadequacy in answering the questions of the elderly. Use the elderly as sources of wisdom. Since they have lived a long life, they have experienced much; they can be our teachers. Give the aged an opportunity to tell their stories. Mary Marks Wilcox has made much of this technique in her paper, "Spiritual Growth in Later Life." Listening actively enables persons to relive their lives, to rewrite the story of meaning which they have constructed through the years. An active listener bestows value upon the story that is told.

The image of reconciliation in the cross of Christ provides an enduring symbol of God's power to create good out of evil, redemption out of destruction. This symbol may be particularly important to the person who feels the weight of despair over a wasted life, broken promise, or failure for which he or she cannot find release. Life has its share of negatives. Persons do get sick; they feel pain, they die; those who are left have their own grief and loneliness with which to deal. Persons must deal with the negatives of their own experience. Jesus, who had to face betrayal, injustice, denial by his followers, aloneness, suffering and death, provides an enduring model for us.

Persons in later years may need help in seeing that more of their life has been spiritual than they were aware of at the time. Some persons have encountered God, experienced grace, and responded with gratitude without ever identifying these experiences with God. The use of ritual with those who are physically or mentally impaired may help recurrent memories of the past. The repetition of words and acts communicates to these persons.

Indeed, all the forms of spirituality may provide helpful guidance to the elderly in the final stage of life. Clergy should develop sensitivities and means of grace to stimulate growth in wholistic forms of spirituality.

NOTES

1. Urban T. Holmes, *Spirituality for Ministry*. (San Francisco: Harper & Row), 1982, p. 12.

2. H. Richard Niebuhr, *The Meaning of Revelation*. (New York: Macmillan), 1967, p. 56.

3. Ibid., pp. 56-57.

4. Paul Maves, *Faith for the Older Years*. (Minneapolis: Augsburg), 1986, p. 24.

5. Ibid., p. 29.

6. Ibid., pp. 37-38.

7. Ibid., pp. 137-141.

8. Erik H. Erikson, *Childhood and Society*. (New York: W.W. Norton), 1963, pp. 268-269.

9. Ibid., p. 269.

10. Erik H. Erikson, Joan M. Erikson & Helen 0. Kivnick, *Vital Involvement In Old Age*. (New York: W.W. Norton), 1986.

Gerontology in Urban and Rural Congregations and Communities

George B. Thomas, DMin

SUMMARY. This is a discussion of urban and rural congregations and communities in service to older persons. Emphasis is on the elderly in an urban Shepherd Center and a rural life center.

There is a paucity of literature on aging as related to the disciplines of theological education. This is especially true of the Black experience in congregations and urban communities.

I come to this subject as an interested participant. I hope to make a contribution to the development and utilization of literature linking gerontology and theological subjects. I must admit that I have been surprised and overwhelmed with the reality that I'm hurtling toward retirement age. In other words, I have been confronted with my own aging.

I had a recent experience that changed my attitude toward the maturing status of older adults. I was invited to accompany a church school class from Shaw Temple A.M.E. Zion Church to the mountains near Boone, North Carolina on a skiing trip. I had always looked on that as a typical "white folk" play time, sliding down a hill on two sticks. I was prevailed upon to try it. After many falls, I graduated to the midrange hill. I could bounce up and down but not side to side, and I could not stop. Three times on the higher hill, I came down into whatever it was that stopped folk at the bottom. At the end of the affair, I bought a button depicting a man on skis, ice flying in front as he stops, but underneath was printed BREAKING OUT. I was "breaking out" at sixty.

George B. Thomas is Professor of Church and Society, Interdenominational Theology Center.

URBAN CONGREGATIONS AND COMMUNITIES

Both the congregation and community must be responsibly sensitive to the needs of older adults and develop both resources and services which will be targeted to meet the concrete needs, resolve the existential problems, and deal with the challenging and sometimes intractable issues, especially with the urban white and non-white poor.

At least two objectives are paramount in this presentation:

1. To cultivate cooperation between the church and agencies in the community to serve the needs of aging citizens.
2. To utilize the resources of the church and the urban area in order to establish goals and set in motion the implementation of the strategies with programs designed to meet needs, to resolve problems, and to deal with issues of aging.

If by 65, older adults have retired, raised their children, and are in reasonably good health, rather than decreasing involvement in the church, there should be broader opportunities for sharing experience and supportive leadership in church activities. Competence, health, energy, and motivation do not have to decline at the crossover into 65 years of age. There are some who become incompetent or senile, maladjusted and dependent, but, for the most part, persons over 65 years of age are relatively free of serious problems.

Since there is so much leisure time at this stage, opportunities for "breaking out" into new adventures in living challenge the church to develop newer ministries and activities for the new age of life styles. Some activities to be explored are: field trips and wider travels, arts and crafts, continuing education, volunteer services in various institutions, and involvement in community and political action. Leisure time provides an opportunity to break out in spirit and into activities of fellowship, outreach, and uplift. In the Black church, it is important to set up several programs, to refer people to supportive institutions and to advocate for new life systems.

Older women represent a very creative potential for vibrant ministries. Women live longer, are less likely to remarry, live alone, and are more supportive in church attendance than men. These resources in skills and strengths are invaluable.

Women have lower incomes than men, and Black women have the lowest incomes of all. There is an obvious correlation between lower income and poorer housing and poorer health. Nevertheless, it is often from the poor, as illustrated in the widow's mite (Mark 12:42), that greater giving to the church becomes a blessed marvel.

A mobile society can isolate the elderly. Often children leave their parents and move distances away leaving many elderly feeling isolated. Others continue some work and make some useful contributions. In fact, the wisdom of the older persons could and should be used. In most cultures throughout history, older people have taught the young and passed on the experiences of living. The church as well as the urban community must discover or recover this responsibility and obligation to develop services and ministries to meet the needs of the aging community. Primary needs focus on the meaning of life and the sense of continued usefulness. What am I to be? What am I to do?

Physical needs include decent and sanitary housing kept in repair and physical therapy. Related needs include transportation of the handicapped/non-ambulatory, help in shopping, homemaking aid and assistance with laundry, home visits, job placement possibilities, day care, and legal services.

Focus on mental health includes meeting psycho-social needs, such as recreation and enrichment opportunities, continuing education, adventures in learning, seminars on aging, elder abuse hotlines, volunteer activities and counseling services. Meeting well-being goals includes cultivating a satisfying philosophy of life, education for life and death, enrichment of living, therapeutic services, a holistic approach, the right to die in dignity, primary nutritional care, balanced meals, nursing assistance, medical services, social monitoring, rehabilitation, and Medicare/Medicaid.

Spiritual needs of the elderly need to be met, such as assurances of God's love, certainty that life is protected, relief from guilt/fear, relief from loneliness, a perspective of life that embraces time/eternity, continuing spiritual growth/new experiences, satisfying status in life, and a feeling of continuing usefulness.

How can the church help older persons accept old age as a blessing from God and a challenge of Christian elderhood? There are several types of programs for meeting needs in the church: worship and congregational services, study classes and group growth experiences, service caring and serving projects, fellowship and creative use of leisure, and general consciousness raising.

Some of these church activities for elders and others may be reviewed.

Focus on worship and congregational services: Choirs, music groups, developing skills, performance, congregational worship, the church family before God, homebound/shut-ins, tape ministry, visitation, Holy Communion, church papers and study materials, adoption by a family, prayer group chains, daily care of others.

Focus on Study and Education: Church school class, Bible and faith studies, community adult school, continuing education, elderhostel, and literacy action.

Focus on Services: Centers for senior adults, day care, health clinics, drop-ins, skills schools, missionary projects at home and abroad, church food store for needy persons, property maintenance chores, care of church buildings, crisis work, camp care, talent banks, personal resources within elderly groups, availability for service (paid or volunteer), telephone reassurances, neighborly calls to keep in touch.

Few studies have focused on Black gerontology and matters of religious participation or informal support. Black participation in religious activities has been examined by Taylor[1] in terms of frequency of attendance, church membership and degree of subjective religiosity. In addition, Deborah Woodworth[2] dealt with Black socio-demographic and religiosity factors as predictors of church-based support. The relation between age and support was modified by the presence of children and church membership. Socio-emotional support during illness was the most prevalent form of reported aid.

The church must strengthen its ministry to the whole needs of aging adults. Both specific and general activities and programs should be implemented based on the existential situation of aging persons in any given time and place.

The urban community provides a variety of services which the church, especially the Black church, should be aware of in its ministry to the elderly. These include a range of personal services, home care, residential facilities (medical, economic, financial and educational), legal and protective resources. These opportunities should be studied by the churches and made available to their elderly members as needed.

As people grow older, there are various human needs to be met: a sense of being, "I am somebody," a sense of belonging and acceptance, a sense of becoming in fellowship, learning, growing and serving. There are needs for encouragement to think positively with a healthy self-esteem. In response to a variety of emotional experiences (guilt, hostility, loneliness, feeling overwhelmed, insecurity), the church should strengthen its ministry to older adults.

In the spirit of the ministry of Jesus (Luke 4:18), the church and community should move to feed the hungry, clothe the naked and proclaim deliverance for the captives. Older persons along with others in congregations can pray, advocate and act to serve the homeless with shelter and food.

The church and community have been surprised and unprepared to give the kind of creative leadership needed to maximize the utilization of the value and service of older adults. A variety of life affirming ministries both within and without the church need to be engaged. Partnership of church and community should plan to deal holistically with needs, problems and issues of older persons.

QUALITY LIVING SERVICE

Quality Living Service (QLS) in Southwest Atlanta is organized on the Shepherd Center Model. We may use it as an example of an active organization which seems to mediate, integrate, and facilitate the acts of ministry in and from the church and as a functional enabler of people of the church and community to benefit from the services and the resources available. It brings together mostly Black churches and urban community organizations to help meet the needs of older persons. It brings together a variety of resources: AARP (American Association of Retired Persons), Barge Road Tenant Association, Ben Hill United Methodist Church, Concerned Black Clergy, Fulton County Council on Aging, Georgia State University Gerontology Center, Ida Prather Y.W.C.A., It's A Woman's World Spa for Women, Morehouse Family Practice Center, Morehouse School of Medicine, NAACP (National Association for the Advancement of Colored People), NPU-P (Neighborhood Planning Unit), NPU-R (Neighborhood Planning Unit), Shepherd Centers, St. Mark A.M.E. Church, Southwest Community Hospital, Spelman College, Trust Company Bank-Ben Hill, Turner Seminary-I.T.C.

Demographics

A demographic study by Atlanta Regional Commission indicates that there are approximately 10,487 persons 65 years old living in the Southwest areas of Atlanta. This study also shows that the number of older persons in this area is rapidly increasing. QLS, to some extent, has eliminated the need for older persons to be bussed out of the area to participate in any recreational, health maintenance, or life enrichment programs.

Goals and Objectives

- To create new program services and develop resources in the Southwest community to sustain the independence and dignity of the people.
- To encourage older persons through educational services, etc., to adopt a life style that includes good health and nutritional practices that help them to maintain optimum levels of usefulness.
- To serve as a clearinghouse and referral unit between the elderly, the physically handicapped, and existing private and governmental agencies.
- Enhance enrichment activities . . . education, recreation and cultural events and socialization, develop "fun" events for seniors.
- Make home delivered meals available to persons who are homebound or who are unable to prepare adequate meals on their own for physical, psychological or sociological reasons. Develop handy-man services program.
- To raise the awareness of seniors . . . "encouraging seniors to volunteer to serve seniors."
- To serve in a general advocacy role to support the elderly and handicapped.

— To work with Marta and other private transportation sources to develop transportation services for the elderly.
— To construct an identifiable multipurpose senior citizen center to carry out the goals and objectives of QLS.

Accomplishments in 1986-87

— QLS is the focal point for services needed by seniors in the Southwest community.
— QLS through volunteer arrangements with the Jewish center coordinates the home sharing program for senior citizens.
— QLS has arranged for medical services and referrals of older persons to Morehouse Family Practice Center.
— QLS members have participated in various seminars, telephone forums, and lectures on subjects of special interest to persons 60 and over.
— QLS sponsors an annual senior citizen fair.
— QLS has provided much of its own funding through the sponsoring of trips, sale of arts and crafts, chances and donations.

Methods to Achieve Goals

— Involve participating members in an active role in the operation of the center through a member organization and volunteer service.
— Offer a part-time health screening, follow-up and referral clinic as a satellite community outreach of the Morehouse Family Practice Medical Program.
— Plan and carry out regularly scheduled seminars, health fairs and lectures on subjects of special interest to persons 60 and over and the disabled.
— Provide entertainment, singing, films, slides, plays and skits, visits to various theaters, and recreational centers.
— Participate in many art forms such as drama, poetry, arts and crafts, painting, drawing, sewing, knitting and quilting.
— Remodel the recreational center at St. Mark A.M.E. Church to meet the needs of QLS Senior Center or establish a new center.
— Develop funding sources such as community, church and indi-

vidual gifts to reduce the amount of needed government dollars.
- Sell wares made by members of the center to create revenue for supplies used for the various activities.
- Building of a strong base of volunteer help is a number one resource priority to serve Southwest Atlanta's aging population.[3]

This is an excellent example of urban congregations and community agencies working together in the Shepherd Center Model to enrich the lives of older persons.

RURAL CONGREGATIONS AND COMMUNITIES

Rural and small-town America has more than its share of elderly persons. Older rural people tend to migrate less while rural youth migrate more, leaving more "old timers" in the country. Small towns and rural areas are becoming places of choice for many elderly who want to move out of cities and, perhaps, out of state. For example, rural towns (1,000 to 2,500) claim 15.4 percent of their population as elderly. This was the largest percentage of elderly of any other rural or urban population. Basically, these older persons live in rural communities with limited resources for coping with their needs.

The map of small-town and rural America is dotted with congregations. Many of these are small in membership and have a higher population of elderly members than the community population. These present great opportunities for ministries by, with and for the elderly. Congregational leaders need training in gerontology in order to develop significant and helpful ministries. They need to know about the community and county resources available. They need, especially, to learn how to involve active elderly in these ministries.

Research into the characteristics and needs of rural elderly provides a sobering yet realistic picture. It differs from the myth of rustic "peace and quiet" along the rural elderly front. The picture shows more shadows than light when comparing the quality of life between rural and urban elderly. A study of each of the following conclusions based on research will provide directions for the development of programs by both congregations and communities to enhance the quality of life of rural elderly:

— On the average the income of rural elderly adults is consistently lower than that of their urban counterparts and a much higher proportion of rural elderly than urban elderly have incomes below the poverty level.
— The rural elderly occupy a disproportionate share of the nation's substandard and dilapidated housing.
— The rural elderly exhibit a larger number of health problems that tend to be more severe in comparison with the urban elderly and that results in a larger percentage of them retiring for health reasons—although this does not necessarily translate into lower life expectancies.
— Studies of the consumption of alcohol indicate a significantly higher percentage of "heavy drinkers" among the rural elderly when compared to their urban counterparts.
— The health and mental health impairments among the elderly are not as readily treated in rural areas; indeed, health and human services are less abundant, less accessible, and more costly to deliver in rural areas than in urban areas.
— Public transportation is more necessary for, but less available to, the rural elderly.
— Studies of the kin relationships of the elderly do not indicate that they are significantly stronger in rural society.[4]

A Field Visit to Hinton Rural Life Center

As part of the Gerontology in Theological Education program, students and faculty participated in an educational field trip to Hinton Rural Life Center, Clay County, North Carolina. The purpose of the visit was to study rural elderly and to visit in their homes and congregations.

The ecumenical Rural Life Center's mission involves working with rural and small-town congregations and communities within Clay County and throughout the Southeast. This mission is carried out through workshops at Hinton and through staff visits at other locations upon request. Aging issues are among its concerns.

Students and faculty evaluations gave high marks to the entire field trip which included a variety of experiences and presentations emphasizing the rural elderly. Local and specific community concerns relating to the elderly of Clay County were presented and discussed by a panel of community residents, including the Director of Hinton Rural Life Center, the Rev. Clay Smith. Dr. Charles Pyles made a presentation on the "Older American's Act" and its impact on rural elderly. The other faculty members present joined Dr. George Thomas in discussing issues of aging as related to the rural elderly. Other highlights of the trip included a presentation by Betsy Styles, Director of the Northside Shepherd's Center, on the cooperative ministry model.

The field trip also provided for personal interaction between the students and the rural elderly. Opportunities were given for visits into the homes and congregations in the county. These personal interactions were perhaps the most significant aspect of the trip. As one student reflected:

> The highlight of my trip was my visit (in a home). A very special thing happened in the little green house by the side of the road. It was as though we had become a family. (She) shared with us her pain, joy, hopes, and dreams — all tied up with the reality of God in her life.

Another student reflecting on lessons learned at Hinton wrote the following:

> In the closing at Hinton, we were asked to share a word or phrase descriptive of our experiences at Hinton. I chose to use the terms "commonality in diversity." By the use of the word commonality, I meant the shared experiences held in common with others. By diversity, I meant the differing histories, experiences, happenings, backgrounds and personalities inherent in each individual.
>
> There was much diversity among the class participants: black, white, African, American, young, middle-aged, older, parent, single, divorced, widowed, etc. There was also the evident diversity between the students and the native/local per-

sons we met: city-bred, rural, poor, well-to-do, mountaineer, flatlander, etc.

With such widespread diversity, commonality in shared experiences and emotions might have seemed difficult to find. It was, however, abundant both within the group and within the student, native and local relationships.

I had expected there to be very little common ground between myself and the rural mountain elderly. However, I found startling commonalities. The eighty-year-old woman I interviewed was very different from me—her life's journey was totally different from mine. Her journey occurred in one very small area; she was born within a mile of her present home; she moved into her home upon marrying. This rural woman, however, shared an artistic sensitivity with me which gave us much commonality.

In retrospect, I have seen that within diversity there is much common ground. It is on this common ground that dialogue and true communication can occur between persons. This in turn reinforces my belief that the young and the old have very much in common, and therefore much to share. Age should not make a difference. Age certainly did not make a difference on our Hinton trip. All of us, whether we are older and rural or younger and city-bred, are, after all, truly one.

NOTES

1. R. J. Taylor, "Religious Participation Among Elderly Blacks," *The Gerontologist*, Vol. 26, (Dec. 1986), pp. 630-636.

2. Deborah L. Woodworth, "Patterned Religious Meanings: Orientations Expressed by a Sample of Elderly Women," *Journal for the Scientific Study of Religion*, Vol. 24, (Dec. 1985), pp. 367-383.

3. From an unpublished manuscript of the Quality Living Service, 1988.

4. Adapted from Raymond Coward and Gary Lee (Eds.), *The Elderly In Rural Society: Every Fourth Elder*, (New York: Springer), 1985, p. 4.

Preaching and Aging

Fred B. Craddock, PhD

SUMMARY. An insightful account of the role of preaching in congregations with various ages, including the elderly, present. It deals with three topics: "Preparation For Preaching," "How One Preaches," and "What One Preaches."

I wish to speak informally on a matter about which, thus far, very little literature is available: Preaching and Aging. Most of the literature on preaching assumes congregations of young and vibrant hearers, and most of the literature on aging has not directly addressed the preacher. In these comments I have in mind not special gatherings of the elderly, but regular congregations, the membership of which is noticeably aging. First, as a general backdrop, listen to three brief paragraphs from a letter I recently received from someone I do not know. The writer is a retiree who has written to me because I teach preaching.

Now that I am retired and experiencing some of the limitations placed on an aging body, I do hear some good preaching, but at other times I just try to hear what the preacher is saying.

Please permit me to suggest that you impress upon preachers that older people do have some loss of hearing. Then impress upon them the fact that more older persons are in their congregations. Tell them they must pronounce and enunciate clearly if we are to continue going to hear them preach. After all, we could be doing other things.

And one other thing, please. Help them understand they were called to give us a message and not just a "three-

---

Fred B. Craddock is Bandy Professor of Preaching and New Testament, Candler School of Theology, Emory University.

pointed" homiletical gem. Many of us are weary before they get to that "third point," which they seem always to call, "Lastly. . . ."

PREPARATION FOR PREACHING

The preacher will want to spend considerable time, especially the first year in a parish, doing exegesis of the congregation. Of course, with increasing knowledge of these people, one's reading will be modified, perhaps even altered. Everything that can be learned about these people is important. But our present concern focuses especially on ages, living arrangements, and networks of relationships. After all, the aging are represented not only by those in the sanctuary on Sunday, not only by those confined at home or in places of special care, but also by younger parishioners who carry in their minds worry over decisions they are making or soon must make about aging members of their families. To be aware of the aging is to be aware of a network of relationships of love, care and sometimes anxiety.

Preparation for preaching involves, of course, spending time with the elderly themselves in their present living contexts. Some younger ministers have never been around older people. A number of medical schools in this country include regular visits with the elderly as part of the training of physicians. This is not simply as a way to get them acquainted with future patients, but because many medical students have never listened to nor observed the elderly in their normal routine. The minister will want to see that other people in the church spend time with them as well. Special attention to patterns of church life will, without calling attention to it, provide for intergenerational activities. Such is not only healthy for all concerned but is, in fact, called for by the very nature of what the church is.

However, the minister will want to beware of overdoing attention to the aging. No one, however in need economically, socially or psychologically, wants to be anyone's project. Ministers, especially, must be careful of this, because there is in the minister's disposition and training a gravitation toward persons with needs. In fact, some pastors seem to love those who need them but are intimidated by those who are healthy, happy, and gainfully employed.

Much information about parishioners can be gotten from them in casual, informal, and even playful ways. For example, much fun and fellowship and community building, as well as understanding, can flow from sharing experience which one might call, "Where did you get your ears?" In groups of ten to fifteen, members are asked to recall the first preachers they heard; those who shaped what one expects preaching to be. A rich and varied background in terms of geography, denominational affiliations, as well as church experiences ranging from shallow to profound, will be revealed in such settings. These are the ears to which the minister will address sermons week after week.

No preparation, by reading or observation, can replace simply taking time to think and reflect. For example, the minister should be impressed by the need for order and predictability in the lives of the aging. All of us need order and management in life, but at this particular stage it becomes increasingly important. What could be more criminal than slipping into the room of an aging person and rearranging the furniture and the pictures on the wall. The resultant disorientation would be devastating. In a large and complex world, now receding from dimming eyes and dulling ears, some measure of control and stability comes by knowing the time and the place. If these are unaccountably altered the feeling is that of being ambushed. The simple change from a clock with hands to a digital timepiece is not really so simple, nor is it welcomed by everyone. There is some sense of disorientation. Neither are unannounced surprises in the order of worship on Sunday. Changes can occur, to be sure, and with appreciation from the elderly, provided preparation for such changes is made.

Or, for another example, let the pastor ponder the word, "alone." What is it to eat alone? Those who devised punishment for criminals long ago realized that one of the most severe forms of punishment is solitary confinement. The Scripture understands this clearly, knowing the enormous burden of loneliness, and therefore, enjoins frequently that attention be given to those members of the community most likely to be caught in its gloomy web, that is, the orphan and the widow. We could add the elderly as well. I think this helps us to understand why Jesus and the early church addressed human need not simply in terms of the need for bread, but the need for the breaking of bread, that is, for companionship at meals.

Or, as a third area of reflection, the minister might give attention to the word, "night." Darkness does not simply introduce the element of fear, though that certainly is present. But add to fear the possibility of falling or the increase of danger from other accidents. Add to that a general melancholy that comes with the setting of the sun. Darkness exaggerates isolation and sense of distance from one's family and friends. A church service, therefore, that is conducted at night, is an entirely different experience from a very similar service scheduled during the day. The thoughtful pastor knows this and prepares messages with these and related factors in mind.

HOW ONE PREACHES

Again let us remind ourselves that we are not thinking of preaching to a gathering of only the elderly, but we are attending to the elderly sitting in regular congregations. Permit me to sketch my remarks here in the form of eight suggestions to the preacher.

1. Clean up one's language. The preacher will want to remove from his or her language all put-downs, such as the too-often-heard expression, "little old ladies in tennis shoes."

2. Vary the moods and tones of sermons. On one Sunday the listeners may be taken on a march, on another Sunday on a parade, on another Sunday on a stroll, and on another Sunday, just a conversation on a park bench. That is to say, enrich the experiences of people through the preaching. Let the preaching give some variety and vitality to life. After all, this will be the central intellectual and social event in the lives of many elderly people. This means, of course, that one will not always preach to the aging. Often one will simply let them listen in. All preachers understand that in fairly large gatherings, a particular audience from within that gathering may be selected, with all other persons there being allowed to overhear. For example, at a funeral the pastor may choose to speak to the neighbors and friends gathered and let the immediate family listen in. By doing so, they are removed from the pressure of having

to pay attention. At a commencement exercise the speaker may choose to address the parents and let the school personnel and the graduating students listen in. As all of us know, those who are not directly addressed often listen most attentively. The suggestion here simply is to include the elderly in making the choice of audience to address and audience to be allowed to overhear what is being addressed to others.

3. Remember that the form of a sermon can orient or disorient the listener. It is not simply the content that can caress or disturb the hearers. It is especially the case in recent years that ministers are experimenting with different forms in their sermons. Instead of the usual, predictable two or three or four points, some ministers, for example, are experimenting with narrative sermons. Others are using dialogical sermons. Some are even using press conference sermons. The minister should know the risk involved here, because for most listeners a change of form is the equivalent of a change of content. Unless the listeners are alerted to the fact that the form will be different, the sermon will be heard as if the content were different. This is not to say that the minister will not on occasion decide to change the form without preparation or announcement ahead of time. This suggestion is simply to alert the minister to the price that will be paid, so that there will not be any loss by default or failure to understand that a change of form in a sermon is like the change of furniture in a room.

4. The minister will think through the importance of appealing to memory. The point here is not that one indulges in more nostalgia or sentimentality if the elderly are present. Memory is a powerful force in anyone's life, regardless of age. Memory gives identity and direction to life. There are all kinds of memories within us. There is the memory of our own personal history. There is the social memory of our family and our immediate connections. There is a national memory. There is a Christian memory. And there is a memory that can be called Adamic, that is, a memory that belongs to all persons simply because of their membership in the human race. Memory is the great, unused resource in preaching. To evoke someone's memory is immediately to have them listen with more complete engagement. Of all the faculties to which a preacher can appeal — intellect, emotion, and will — there is none to which the

message can appeal more powerfully than that of memory. All great preaching has understood this.

5. Remember to include the aging in the population of your sermons. Good preaching always has a large cast of characters. It is not simply about ideas, but it is about preaching. The range of people found in good pastoral preaching includes rich and poor, young and old, white and black, male and female, Hispanics, Orientals, all types, from all positions in life. Unless the preacher is very intentional about this, it is likely that stories in sermons will be too frequently about grandchildren or about the time when the minister played football in high school. Such preaching becomes exclusive rather than inclusive. This suggestion is simply to remember the elderly when you begin to build in the analogies and the illustrative material in the sermons.

6. Build into the messages some anticipation. The element of anticipation is handled by the form or the movement of the sermon. Like its first cousin, the short story, good sermons cause the listeners to anticipate, to predict, to run ahead of the speaker, to adjust, and finally, to arrive at a conclusion. Poor preaching says the whole thing in summary in the introduction and then spends the rest of the time allotted explaining, exhorting and pushing what has already been said. In order to create anticipation one must exercise restraint and allow the listener to arrive at the conclusion at the time the speaker does. Anticipation is the greatest single source of pleasure anyone has. The pastor builds it into every act of ministry wherever possible. For example, whenever making pastoral calls the pastor doesn't just show up on Thursday afternoon to visit with the elderly. The pastor calls on Monday morning and asks permission to come by on Thursday afternoon. By doing so, the whole week has been filled with anticipation, and the value of the visit has been multiplied many times over. What is being suggested here is simply to make sure that the sermon has anticipation built into it.

7. The preacher can trust the aging to apply the sermons appropriately to themselves without their being told that this is for them or that they are very similar in behavior or situation to those being discussed in the sermon. I have written elsewhere about a former student of mine who preached in a home for the elderly and used as her sermon text the story in Mark 10 about Jesus blessing the little

children. It was a striking use of a text about children in a home for the elderly. In the text the disciples try to prevent the mothers from bringing their babies to Jesus, apparently feeling that they were in the way and could not actually contribute anything to the occasion. Jesus, however, rebuked his disciples and asked for the children to be brought. The sermon consisted of the young preacher asking the question, "Why do you suppose the disciples did not want the children brought to Jesus? Was it because they could not contribute, could not sing, could not preach, could not read the text, had no money? Was it because they actually were a problem for others, that they had to be cared for, that care for them kept other people from engaging fully in the life of the church?" When she began to probe these questions as to why the little children would be hindered in being a part of the community around Jesus, these elderly people began to nod in agreement, because they knew the preacher was not talking about small children, the preacher was talking about them. When, therefore, the preacher said, "The words of Jesus permit the children to come to me," they all were pleased and smiled. It was not necessary for the young preacher to say, "Aren't many of you very much like those young children today, unable to do this, unable to do that, having no money to give? Aren't many of you like those children today, having to be cared for, keeping others from full participation because they must attend to your needs?" To have done that would have been cruel and inhuman. As it was, the preacher never ceased talking about the children. The listeners made the transfer to themselves. Let all of us learn from this. Aging people have the capacity to bring appropriate messages from our sermons into their lives without always having us direct attention to them.

8. Let the preacher release his or her sense of humor, and thereby release the sense of humor in others. A sense of humor is really a sense of freedom. Many among the older parishioners are more free than they have ever been. More able to laugh than they ever have. Now that the children are grown, now that the obligations of a pressure job are over, many of these have a sense of humor that they never experienced nor realized they had until now. They enjoy having that laughter released, and lest anyone wonder about it, laughter and the free play of a sense of humor are not inappropriate to the

sanctuary. They honor God and speak more generously of a sense of grace and freedom before God than many of our other explanations about grace and freedom.

WHAT ONE PREACHES

It is important to keep in mind the idea expressed in the letter earlier: We come to church to hear a message. Sometimes preachers deprive persons of the Gospel for the strangest reasons. For example, before the rich, one can easily forget their areas of poverty. Before the poor, one can make them even poorer by failing to share with them the Gospel. Before the young, the preacher can be so full of warnings about errant ways of life that there is for them no good news. Before the aging, one can become sentimental, or so preoccupied with issues of aging that one forgets that they came to hear the Gospel which had sustained them through all their years.

Basic to all effective preaching is trust. To build a relationship of trust one needs to share what is held in common with the hearers, and among those things are Scripture, prayer, and praise. From these one can move to the edges of application to particular issues. But first must come the trust. Not simply standing in common before God in trust, but trust of each other because with each other we have shared the tradition which called us to be together.

In dealing with the deceased, whether they be persons who are described in Scripture or in history or in a local obituary, the preacher will speak with honor and with respect. One's listeners can conclude from the way we treat the dead how they will be regarded after they are gone. What is involved here is not simply some old slogan about speaking kindly of the dead, but rather, a continuation of that element of trust which is built when one hears the preacher talk with understanding, insight, and respect about the deceased. In more minds than a minister may imagine the question arises, How will the preacher speak of me after I am gone?

Concerning preaching on the hereafter, one will neither neglect the subject nor give it undue attention. As with any slice of the general population, the aging have quite a range of views and interest in the matter of life after death. The Scripture provides a wide variety of accents and degrees of interest in the subject. If these are shared, then all the listeners will be nourished. Certainly the preacher will not engage in any carnival pictures of the hereafter, extending himself/herself beyond the bounds of the Scripture, itself, which treats this matter, as well as other matters, in noticeably brief fashion, with an economy of words. What we do not know, we do not know.

In all preaching the sermons will affirm the value of life apart from the criterion of productivity. Many of the aging themselves are searching for new ground on which to stand now that their most productive years are past. Again, this is a subject important for all of one's hearers and not simply the aging. A great deal of life's value is in terms of relationships and in the love of God. The preacher, therefore, will proclaim the impartiality of God, whose Son and reign take no note of difference in people, physical, economic, mental, or even moral. God's love affirms the value of every person, and the healthy church affirms that, in a network of relationships that is blind to many of the differences which become exaggerated in other contexts.

The preacher will want to be honest in considering the grim realities of life. There is, after all, a kind of freedom, a recognition of good news in the clear facing of the realities of health, work, play, suffering and death. New life can begin with the embrace of necessity, with an honest confronting the question of "What do you do when there is nothing you can do?" False hopes and illusory alternatives are finally quite cruel and unfair.

And this includes discussions of death. Death is, of course, on the agenda of every preacher, but not every preacher has spent time reflecting upon and developing sensitivity to the complexity of the subject. For instance, let the preacher think about the context in which death occurs. In rural areas death is viewed more as a part of life. In that particular context, the death of animals, the death of plants and trees and persons are all observed in a pattern of consistency and, painful as it is, find a kind of general acceptance. In cities, on the other hand, it seems that only violent deaths receive visibility. The natural deaths are not newsworthy and therefore are tucked away in the fine print of an obituary column on the last page. Or again, it is important that the preacher be aware that the major point of pain is not in the contemplation of one's own death but in the loss of those we love most. And again, the preacher will want to reflect upon the fact that with the increase of the average life span more and more of the aging must survive the deaths of some of their children. Hardly any pain surpasses that. To bury one's parents hurts enough. To bury one's children hurts too much.

And finally, let the preacher keep challenges before the aging. I recall visiting with a pastor in a nursing home some years ago. Instead of moving from wheelchair to wheelchair and from room to room giving a touch and a prayer for relief of discomfort or pain, he called the roll of these people as though they were his staff. Each one of his members in the nursing home had assignments to carry out and he called them to responsibility. One of the members was physically able to call in the rooms of those who were not able to move about. Others were responsible for praying for the sick of the church. Others were responsible for making phone calls reminding members of church activities. As so the list of duties extended. It struck me, at first, as a bit demanding of these elderly people until I realized that it was life-giving and they loved every minute of it. They are not to be let off the hook, nor do they want to be. There is volunteer work enough and to spare. Even the confined can pray or make phone calls. The ambulatory can call upon those who are bedridden. It takes a little time, of course, to work out such a program, and it takes a little imagination to do it in such a way that there is ministry with delight for everyone. But the whole church will be blessed and none will be more blessed than those elderly people whose gifts continue to be shared and who insist, "I came not to be ministered unto, but to minister."